BioCritiques

Bloom's BioCritiques

MAYA ANGELOU

Edited and with an introduction by
Harold Bloom
Sterling Professor of the Humanities
Yale University

CHELSEA HOUSE PUBLISHERS
Philadelphia

Printed and bound in the United States of America

10 9 8 7 6 5 4 3 2

Library of Congress Cataloging-in-Publication Data

Maya Angelou / edited and with an introduction by Harold Bloom.
    p. cm. – (Bloom's biocritiques)
Includes bibliographical references and index.
    ISBN 0-7910-6177-9
    1. Angelou, Maya. 2. African American women civil rights
workers—Biography. 3. Authors, American—20th century—Biography.
4. African American women authors—Biography. 5. African American
authors—Biography. 6. African Americans in literature. I. Bloom,
Harold. II. Series
    PS3551.N464 Z763 2002
    818'.5409—dc21
                                    2002002189

Chelsea House Publishers
1974 Sproul Road, Suite 400
Broomall, PA 19008-0914

http://www.chelseahouse.com

Contributing editor: Rachel Thomas

Layout by EJB Publishing Services

CONTENTS

User's Guide

These volumes are designed to introduce the reader to the life and work of the world's literary masters. Each volume begins with Harold Bloom's essay "The Work in the Writer" and a volume-specific introduction also written by Professor Bloom. Following these unique introductions is an engaging biography that discusses the major life events and important literary accomplishments of the author under consideration.

Furthermore, each volume includes an original critique that not only traces the themes, symbols, and ideas apparent in the author's works, but strives to put those works into cultural and historical perspectives. In addition to the original critique is a brief selection of significant critical essays previously published on the author and his or her works followed by a concise and informative chronology of the writer's life. Finally, each volume concludes with a bibliography of the writer's works, a list of additional readings, and an index of important themes and ideas.

HAROLD BLOOM

The Work in the Writer

Literary biography found its masterpiece in James Boswell's *Life of Samuel Johnson*. Boswell, when he treated Johnson's writings, implicitly commented upon Johnson as found in his work, even as in the great critic's life. Modern instances of literary biography, such as Richard Ellmann's lives of W. B. Yeats, James Joyce, and Oscar Wilde, essentially follow in Boswell's pattern.

That the writer somehow is in the work, we need not doubt, though with William Shakespeare, writer-of-writers, we almost always need to rely upon pure surmise. The exquisite rancidities of the Problem Plays or Dark Comedies seem to express an extraordinary estrangement of Shakespeare from himself. When we read or attend *Troilus and Cressida* and *Measure for Measure*, we may be startled by particular speeches of Ulysses in the first play, or of Vincentio in the second. These speeches, of Ulysses upon hierarchy or upon time, or of Duke Vincentio upon death, are too strong either for their contexts or for the characters of their speakers. The same phenomenon occurs with Parolles, the military impostor of *All's Well That Ends Well*. Utterly disgraced, he nevertheless affirms: "Simply the thing I am/Shall make me live."

In Shakespeare, more even than in his peers, Dante and Cervantes, meaning always starts itself again through excess or overflow. The strongest of Shakespeare's creatures—Falstaff, Hamlet, Iago, Lear, Cleopatra—have an exuberance that is fiercer than their plays can contain. If Ben Jonson was at all correct in his complaint that "Shakespeare wanted art," it could have been only in a sense that he may not have intended. Where do the personalities of Falstaff or Hamlet touch a limit? What was it in Shakespeare that made the two parts of *Henry IV* and *Hamlet* into "plays unlimited"? Neither Falstaff nor Hamlet will be stopped: their wit, their beautiful, laughing speech, their intensity of being—all these are virtually infinite.

In what ways do Falstaff and Hamlet manifest the writer in the work? Evidently, we can never know, or know enough to answer with any authority. But what would happen if we reversed the question, and asked: How did the work form the writer, Shakespeare?

Of Shakespeare's inwardness, his biography tells us nothing. And yet, to an astonishing extent, Shakespeare created our inwardness. At the least, we can speculate that Shakespeare so lived his life as to conceal the depths of his nature, particularly as he rather prematurely aged. We do not have Shakespeare on Shakespeare, as any good reader of the Sonnets comes to realize: they do not constitute a key that unlocks his heart. No sequence of sonnets could be less confessional or more powerfully detached from the poet's self.

The German poet and universal genius, Goethe, affords a superb contrast to Shakespeare. Of Goethe's life, we know more than everything; I wonder sometimes if we know as much about Napoleon or Freud or any other human being who ever has lived, as we know about Goethe. Everywhere, we can find Goethe in his work, so much so that Goethe seems to crowd the writing out, just as Byron and Oscar Wilde seem to usurp their own literary accomplishments. Goethe, cunning beyond measure, nevertheless invested a rival exuberance in his greatest works that could match his personal charisma. The sublime outrageousness of the Second Part of *Faust*, or of the greater lyric and meditative poems, form a Counter-Sublime to Goethe's own daemonic intensity.

Goethe was fascinated by the daemonic in himself; we can doubt that Shakespeare had any such interests. Evidently, Shakespeare abandoned his acting career just before he composed *Measure for Measure* and *Othello*. I surmise that the egregious interventions by Vincentio and Iago displace the actor's energies into a new kind of mischief-making, a fresh opening to a subtler playwriting-within-the-play.

But what had opened Shakespeare to this new awareness? The answer is the work in the writer, *Hamlet* in Shakespeare. One can go further: it was not so much the play, *Hamlet*, as the character Hamlet, who changed Shakespeare's art forever.

Hamlet's personality is so large and varied that it rivals Goethe's own. Ironically Goethe's Faust, his Hamlet, has no personality at all, and is as colorless as Shakespeare himself seems to have chosen to be. Yet nothing could be more colorful than the Second Part of *Faust*, which is peopled by an astonishing array of monsters, grotesque devils, and classical ghosts.

A contrast between Shakespeare and Goethe demonstrates that in each—but in very different ways—we can better find the work in the person, than we can discover that banal entity, the person in the work. Goethe to many of his contemporaries, seemed to be a mortal god. Shakespeare, so far as we know, seemed an affable, rather ordinary fellow, who aged early and became somewhat withdrawn. Yet Faust, though Mephistopheles battles for his soul, is hardly worth the trouble unless you take him as an idea and not as a person. Hamlet is nearly every-idea-in-one, but he is precisely a personality and a person.

Would Hamlet be so astonishingly persuasive if his father's ghost did not haunt him? Falstaff is more alive than Prince Hal, who says that the devil haunts him in the shape of an old fat man. Three years before composing the final *Hamlet*, Shakespeare invented Falstaff, who then never ceased to haunt his creator. Falstaff and Hamlet may be said to best represent the work in the writer, because their influence upon Shakespeare was prodigious. W.H. Auden accurately observed that Falstaff possesses infinite energy: never tired, never bored, and absolutely both witty and happy until Hal's rejection destroys him. Hamlet too has infinite energy, but in him it is more curse than blessing.

Falstaff and Hamlet can be said to occupy the roles in Shakespeare's invented world that Sancho Panza and Don Quixote possess in Cervantes's. Shakespeare's plays from 1610 on (starting with *Twelfth Night*) are thus analogous to the Second Part of Cervantes's epic novel. Sancho and the Don overtly jostle Cervantes for authorship in the Second Part, even as Cervantes battles against the impostor who has pirated a continuation of his work. As a dramatist, Shakespeare manifests the work in the writer more indirectly. Falstaff's prose genius is revived in the scapegoating of Malvolio by Maria and Sir Toby Belch, while Falstaff's darker insights are developed by Feste's melancholic wit. Hamlet's intellectual resourcefulness, already deadly, becomes poisonous in Iago and in Edmund. Yet we have not crossed into the deeper abysses of the work in the writer in later Shakespeare.

No fictive character, before or since, is Falstaff's equal in self-trust. Sir John, whose delight in himself is contagious, has total confidence both in his self-awareness and in the resources of his language. Hamlet, whose self is as strong, and whose language is as copious, nevertheless distrusts both the self and language. Later Shakespeare is, as it were, much under the influence both of Falstaff and of Hamlet, but they tug him in opposite directions. Shakespeare's own copiousness of language is well-nigh incredible: a vocabulary in excess of twenty-one thousand words, almost eighteen hundred of which he coined himself. And of his word-hoard, nearly half are used only once each, as though the perfect setting for each had been found, and need not be repeated. Love for language and faith in language are Falstaffian attributes. Hamlet will darken both that love and that faith in Shakespeare, and perhaps the Sonnets can best be read as Falstaff and Hamlet counterpointing against one another.

Can we surmise how aware Shakespeare was of Falstaff and Hamlet, once they had played themselves into existence? *Henry IV, Part I* appeared in six quarto editions during Shakespeare's lifetime; *Hamlet* possibly had four. Falstaff and Hamlet were played again and again at the Globe, but Shakespeare knew also that they were being read, and he must have had contact with some of those readers. What would it have been like to discuss Falstaff or Hamlet with one of their early readers (presumably also part of their audience at the Globe), if you were the creator of such demiurges? The question would seem nonsensical to most Shakespeare scholars, but then these days they tend to be either ideologues or moldy figs. How can we recover the uncanniness of Falstaff and of Hamlet, when they now have become so familiar?

A writer's influence upon himself is an unexplored problem in criticism, but such an influence is never free from anxieties. The biocritical problem (which this series attempts to explore) can be divided into two areas, difficult to disengage fully. Accomplished works affect the author's life, and also affect her subsequent writings. It is simpler for me to surmise the effect of *Mrs. Dalloway* and *To the Lighthouse* upon Woolf's late *Between the Acts*, than it is to relate Clarissa Dalloway's suicide and Lily Briscoe's capable endurance in art to the tragic death and complex life of Virginia Woolf.

There are writers whose lives were so vivid that they seem sometimes to obscure the literary achievement: Byron, Wilde, Malraux, Hemingway. But most major Western writers do not live that exuberantly, and the greatest of all, Shakespeare, sometimes appears to have adopted the personal mask of colorlessness. And yet there are heroes of literature who struggled titanically with their own eras—Tolstoy, Milton, Victor Hugo—who nevertheless matter more for their works than their lives.

There are great figures—Emily Dickinson, Wallace Stevens, Willa Cather—who seem to have had so little of the full intensity of life when compared to the vitality of their work, that we might almost speak of the work in the work, rather than even of the work in a person. Emily Brontë might well be the extreme instance of such a visionary, surpassing William Blake in that one regard.

I conclude this general introduction to a series of literary bio-critiques by stating a tentative formula or principle for gauging the many ways in which the work influences the person and her subsequent, later work. Our influence upon ourselves is always related to the Shakespearean invention of self-overhearing, which I have written about in several other contexts. Life, as well as poetry and prose, is overheard rather than simply heard. The writer listens to herself as though she were somebody else, and the will to change begins to operate. The forces that live in us include the prior work we have done, and the dreams and waking visions that evade our dismissals.

HAROLD BLOOM

Introduction

Maya Angelou is beyond literary criticism, so I compose this brief introduction not as a literary critic but as an admirer of a great personality. An imposing and majestic six-footer, she has manifested an indomitable spirit and benign will in her most famous book, *I Know Why the Caged Bird Sings*, the first volume of her ongoing autobiography.

Ms. Angelou is much the most popular contemporary poet in the United States, a testimony both to her exuberance and to her shrewdness in making no demands upon her readers. She is a passionately *sincere* poet, whose purpose is to inspire her audience to keep going. Her best efforts are her ballads, which link her to folk traditions.

Recently, Ms. Angelou has ventured on her own line of Hallmark greeting cards, table runners, pillows and related items. Her defense of this enterprise seems to me persuasive:

> I was once told I shouldn't do it because the person said: "You are the people's poet, the most popular poet in the United States, and you shouldn't trivialize your work." So when I hung up the phone and thought about it, I said: "If I'm the people's poet, then my work should be in the people's hands. There are many people who will never buy a book but who would buy a card."

Libraries are now named after Maya Angelou, and *The New York Times* describes her as a "cultural diva," akin to Oprah Winfrey. The *Times* also hailed Ms. Angelou's poem for Bill Clinton's first inauguration, in 1993, as possessing "Whitmanian amplitudes."

There will soon be a *Maya Angelou Cook Book*. It is accurate to describe Ms. Angelou as a National Institution.

CINDY DYSON

Biography of Maya Angelou

Eating Sound

The car's motor lulled Angelou nearly to sleep as she and her friends moved deeper into the Ghana countryside. Without warning, a sudden feeling of terror washed over her and she snapped alert.

"Stop the car!" she demanded.

Angelou flung herself out. She stood staring across a long, sturdy bridge spanning a river.

"I could not explain my behavior," Angelou said. "I only knew that the possibility of riding across that bridge so terrified me that had the driver refused to stop, I would have jumped from the still-moving car." She instead began to walk alone over the bridge.

Her host on the trip, a Mr. Adadevo, indulged Angelou, meeting her with the car on the other side. He asked her why she refused to ride in the car. She shook her head, unable to explain. To her surprise, Mr. Adadevo then stated that the bridge had been infamously dangerous in past centuries. The people who lived near it had always insisted on walking across it.

Angelou tucked her strange feelings away and got back in the car. They were headed toward the small town of Keta. As the car approached a curve, another unexpected, unexplainable feeling swept over her. She knew that with this curve, she would see the ocean surf.

"I swallowed the knots in my throat over and over and wondered if I was losing my mind," Angelou remembered. "What did that bridge and the sea's encroachment on Keta have to do with me?"

3

Angelou had been in Africa four years. Although she hadn't come to search for her roots, she often found herself wondering, as she explored strange villages, "Is this the home of my ancestors? Was my great-great-great-grandmother living here when they took her?"

Mr. Adadevo parked and led Angelou and her friends to the town marketplace—a voice drew her attention. Angelou looked to find an older woman, tall and thin, speaking to her in Ewe, a language she didn't understand.

"When she raised her head, I nearly fell back down the steps: she had the wide face and slanted eyes of my grandmother," Angelou recalled. "Her lips were large and beautifully shaped like my grandmother's, and her cheekbones were high like those of my grandmother."

The woman reached out and patted Angelou's cheeks, studying her face, then lifted both arms, and laced her fingers on top of her head. She began to rock from side to side and a pitiful moan left her lips.

The woman then took Angelou's hand and led her to another stall, where she spoke to the woman who owned it. This woman too looked closely at Angelou, then lifted and laced her hands, moaning and rocking. The women led Angelou to another stall and another, each time speaking to the proprietress, who each time, after some scrutiny, began moaning and rocking.

"Their distress was contagious, and my lack of understanding made it especially so," Angelou recollected. "I wanted to apologize, but I didn't know what I would ask pardon for."

Confused, Angelou turned to Mr. Adadevo and said, "You must tell me what's happening."

Mr. Adadevo understood a little. During the time of the slave trade, nearly every inhabitant of Keta was killed or captured. The only ones to escape were children who hid in the brush. They saw their parents beaten and chained. They saw parents bash infants' heads against trees so they would not be taken into bondage. While many children were adopted by a nearby village, they remembered what happened to them and told their children, who in turn told their children.

"They have heard the stories often," Mr. Adadevo said of the current villagers, "and the deeds are still as fresh as if they happened during their lifetimes. And you, Sister, you look so much like them, even the tone of your voice is like theirs. They are sure you are descended from those stolen mothers and fathers. That is why they mourn. Not for you but for their lost people."

Angelou looked at these black Africans. Could they really be her people? At 37 years old, had she at last found her stolen home?

"The women wept and I wept," Angelou remembered. "I too cried for the lost people, their ancestors and mine. But I was also weeping with a curious joy. . . .Although separated from our languages, our families, and our customs, we had dared to continue to live. We had crossed the unknowable oceans in chains. . . . Through the centuries of despair and dislocation, we had been creative, because we faced down death by daring to hope."

Maya Angelou was on the cusp of a literary career when she visited Keta in 1965. She had begun to write, but was not yet famous. She was planning to return to America, but had no firm plans outside of that. She had seen a good bit of the world, but hadn't found her place in it yet. She was a singer and dancer, a mother, a friend, and a journalist, yet so many talents, so much wisdom seemed buried with her confusion, longing, and a past she could not shake loose.

Throughout her work and life runs the thread of the self-knowledge that she acquired, in part, that day in Keta's marketplace. There is a unity in the human spirit that transcends time and distance, experience, and appearance. This is the drum Maya Angelou beats—as an autobiographer, a poet, a lecturer, an actress, a director, a singer, a professor: —We are more alike than unalike.

Marguerite Annie Johnson was born on April 4, 1928, in St. Louis, Missouri, into a family on the edge. Her mother, Vivian Baxter, worked as a card dealer in a gambling parlor. Her father, Bailey Johnson Sr., worked as a doorman. A year before, the couple had had their first child, Bailey Jr. Bailey couldn't pronounce the name Marguerite and took to calling his new sister Mya Sister—and eventually just Maya. The nickname stuck for her entire life.

Vivian and Bailey Sr. divorced when Maya was just three. Their father took Maya and Bailey to the train station, fastened cards around their wrists that read, "To Whom It May Concern," listed the children's names and the fact that they were traveling to a Mrs. Annie Henderson in Stamps, Arkansas, and sent them off alone halfway across the country.

Mrs. Henderson, Bailey Sr.'s mother, owned a general store in the small rural town. She lived in the back of the store with her son, Willie. America was in the midst of the Great Depression, and small farming towns such as Stamps were especially hard hit.

In depressed and segregated Stamps, as in most Southern towns, blacks and whites lived in separate worlds. Black families lived in the Quarters, separated from the white neighborhoods by the Red River and the train tracks. Most of the black men made their living farming, either on their own small places or on one of the large cotton plantations nearby, while the women often took in washing or worked as maids.

Annie Henderson stood out. She towered above the children, standing six feet four inches tall. She had a wide face and cinnamon-hued skin. She was one of Stamps's few black entrepreneurs. She and Willie, who was paralyzed on his right side and walked with difficulty on a cane, ran the store together, selling to Stamps's black residents.

One of the first things Maya learned about life in Stamps was that white people were not to be trusted. Mrs. Henderson taught her to never speak to a white person; to do so was to risk one's life—not that she was ever afforded much opportunity to do so. White people didn't come to the Quarters and blacks didn't go into white neighborhoods except to work. Maya thought white people were more like ghosts than people.

"White folks couldn't be people," Maya thought, "because their feet were too small, their skin too white and see-throughy, and they didn't walk on the balls of their feet the way people did—they walked on their heels like horses."

As Maya and Bailey grew, Mrs. Henderson had them help in the store. Maya ladled out flour, corn, and sugar into paper bags for customers. After closing time, she'd feed the chickens and pigs.

Annie Henderson was a devoted churchgoer and Willie was the superintendent of the Sunday school at the Christian Methodist Episcopal Church. Maya and Bailey had to sit on the hard benches at church for six long hours as each Sunday service dragged on. While she loved the poetry of the sermons and the gospel music, Maya often tuned out and daydreamed.

As a strict caretaker, Mrs. Henderson insisted that Maya and Bailey wash at the well, study their Sunday school lessons, and say their prayers every evening. They addressed adults as Mrs. or Mr., or as Auntie so-and-so or Uncle or Sister or Brother.

From the time of her arrival, Maya believed her mother's death was the reason why she and Bailey had been sent away and furthermore, why she had never heard from her parents. Maya pictured her mother lying in a coffin, her black hair spread on a small white pillow. She couldn't remember her mother's face and saw only a brown circle with the word "mother" imprinted across it.

But when she was six, both her mother and her father sent Christmas gifts. Maya got a tea set and a doll with blue eyes and painted blond hair. Her father sent a picture of himself.

"I didn't know what Bailey received, but after I opened my boxes I went out to the backyard behind the chinaberry tree," Maya remembered. "The day was cold and the air as clear as water. Frost was still on the bench but I sat down and cried. I looked up and Bailey was coming from the outhouse, wiping his eyes. . . . The gifts opened the door to questions that neither of us wanted to ask. Why did they send us away? and What did we do so wrong? So Wrong?"

One day when Maya was seven, her father unexpectedly pulled up in front of the store in a big De Soto. He was big and handsome and talked, Maya thought, like a white man. He had come to take Maya and Bailey to live with their mother, who had moved to St. Louis. Maya was terrified of meeting the woman who had sent her away. She was afraid her mother wouldn't like her, wouldn't want to keep her.

But as soon as Maya met her mother, she fell in love. Vivian was light-skinned, pretty, and fun. She seemed the opposite of Maya, who was tall with big feet and a gap between her front teeth.

"To describe my mother would be to write about a hurricane in its perfect power," Maya said. "I knew immediately why she had sent me away. She was too beautiful to have children. . . . Bailey on his part fell instantly and forever in love. I saw his eyes shining like hers; he had forgotten the loneliness and the nights when we had cried together because we were 'unwanted children.'"

To Maya, St. Louis was a foreign country. The streets were paved, coal dust clouded the air, and mammoth brick buildings crowded the streets. The schools were different, too. Bailey and Maya were far ahead of their peers and quickly moved ahead a grade.

When Maya and Bailey moved in with their mother, who was still working part-time as a card dealer, they enjoyed more luxury than they'd ever dreamed of. Vivian's home was large and elegant. Maya had her own room, lots of store-bought clothes, a radio, and spending money for books. Vivian even had her take dance lessons, and Maya would often entertain guests by showing off the new steps she was learning.

Although Maya and Bailey loved their mother, they were afraid of her, too—afraid that if they did anything wrong, she'd send them away again. Bailey began to stutter under the pressure, and Maya began to have nightmares. Sometimes her dreams were so bad that Vivian would let Maya climb into bed with her and her boyfriend. Her boyfriend at the time, a Mr. Freeman, lived with the family and was a foreman for the Southern Pacific Railway.

One morning Maya's mother woke up early and went to run an errand, leaving Maya and Mr. Freeman alone in bed together. Taking advantage of the situation, Mr. Freeman molested Maya that morning in her mother's bed. Afterward, "He held me so softly that I wished he wouldn't ever let me go," Maya said. "I felt at home. From the way he was holding me I knew he'd never let me go or let anything bad ever happen to me. This was probably my real father and we had found each other at last."

While pulling on his clothes, Mr. Freeman told Maya that if she told anyone what they had done, he would kill her brother Bailey.

Maya recoiled. "What had we done?" she wondered.

For weeks afterward, Mr. Freeman ignored Maya, which left her confused. To pass her time, Maya began reading more, especially enjoying Horatio Alger stories. She spent Saturdays at the library, "breathing in the world of penniless shoeshine boys who, with goodness and perseverance, became rich, rich men. . . . The little princesses who were mistaken for maids, and the long-lost children mistaken for waifs, became more real to me than our house, our mother, our school or Mr. Freeman."

One late-spring Saturday, when they were in the house alone, Mr. Freeman called to Maya. He was sitting in his chair by the radio. Maya tried to back away but he grabbed her arm, turned up the radio, and pulled her between his legs. Mr. Freeman raped eight-year-old Maya there in the living room. Maya thought she would die. She lost consciousness and woke up to Mr. Freeman washing her in the bathtub. Again he threatened to kill Bailey if she told anyone.

Maya climbed into bed, hiding her blood-stained underwear under the mattress. That night, as her temperature climbed with an infection, Mr. Freeman packed and left.

The next day, when Vivian changed her damp sheets, Maya's hidden underwear fell at her mother's feet. Vivian rushed Maya to the hospital, where Maya told Bailey what had happened. Bailey promptly told Grandmother Baxter, Vivian's mother. Grandmother Baxter and her four sons were known as tough and politically connected. Within hours, Mr. Freeman had been arrested.

The courtroom was packed when Mr. Freeman's trial began. Maya, wrapped in her heavy blue winter coat despite the hot Missouri summer, took the witness stand.

> "Did the accused try to touch you before the time he or rather you say he raped you?" the defense attorney asked.
>
> I couldn't say yes and tell them how he had loved me once for a few minutes and how he had held me close. . . . And Mother, who thought I was such a good girl, would be so disappointed. But most important, there was Bailey. I had kept a big secret from him. . . .
>
> Everyone in the court knew that the answer had to be No. Everyone except Mr. Freeman and me. . . . I said No.
>
> The lie lumped in my throat and I couldn't get air. How I despised the man for making me lie.

Mr. Freeman was sentenced to one year and one day in jail, but his lawyer got him released that afternoon. He was found kicked to death and dumped behind a slaughterhouse shortly afterward.

The news shook Maya. "A man was dead because I lied," she thought. "Where was the balance in that? One lie surely wouldn't be worth a man's life. . . . Just my breath, carrying my words out, might poison people and they'd curl up and die like the black fat slugs that only pretended. . . . I had to stop talking."

Silence was easy enough, Maya discovered:

> I discovered that to achieve perfect personal silence all I had to do was to attach myself leechlike to sound. I began to listen to everything. . . . I walked into rooms where people were laughing, their voices hitting the walls like stones and I simply stood still— in the midst of the riot of sound. After a minute or two, silence would rush into the room from its hiding place because I had eaten up all the sounds.

At first her family thought her silence was temporary. Nobody mentioned the rape or Freeman's death, thinking Maya would forget and return to normal.

When Maya remained mute for weeks, her family didn't know how to react.

"When I refused to be the child they knew and accepted me to be, I was called impudent and my muteness sullenness. . . .For a while I was punished for being so uppity that I wouldn't speak; and then came the thrashings, given by any relative who felt himself offended."

Three months after the trial, Maya and Bailey were put on a train back to Stamps. Maya never knew if her mother sent her back or if Annie had asked that the children come back.

Maya didn't care.

DEEPER SHADES

Nothing happened in Stamps and nobody expected anything to happen. Maya felt safe there, for if nothing happened, nothing more would happen to her, either. She did not relax her vow of silence, and only Annie and Uncle Willie knew the trauma that had led to Maya's refusal to speak. Customers and friends had to find their own answers to the question of Maya's silence.

And so Maya continued during her first year back in Stamps until she met Mrs. Bertha Flowers, the "aristocrat of Black Stamps." Mrs. Flowers wore printed dresses and flowered hats. She spoke formally and quietly. She was rich by comparison, and Maya idolized her. One day Mrs. Flowers asked Maya to carry her purchases home. Maya rushed to change into a school dress and followed Mrs. Flowers.

"I hear you're doing very good schoolwork, Marguerite, but that it's all written," Mrs. Flowers said as they walked along a little path by the road. "The teachers report that they have trouble getting you to talk in class."

Maya hung back, silent.

"Now no one is going to make you talk—possibly no one can," Mrs. Flowers continued. "But bear in mind, language is man's way of communicating with his fellow man and it is language alone which separates him from the lower animals. . . .Words mean more than what is set down on paper. It takes the human voice to infuse them with the shades of deeper meaning."

Maya had never thought of words this way. When the two reached Mrs. Flowers's house, she invited Maya in for cookies and lemonade. Maya was astonished to be asked in and astonished when Mrs. Flowers gave her some books that she said must be read aloud. She told Maya to read each sentence in as many different ways as possible to see how her voice could subtly change the meaning. Then she read from *A Tale of Two Cities*.

"She opened the first page and I heard poetry for the first time in my life," Maya remembered. "Her voice slid in and curved down through and over the words. She was nearly singing."

Maya, with help from Mrs. Flowers and books, began to emerge from her silence.

At first she'd just retreat to the corner of the store and recite poetry by herself. Often she'd become so engrossed that customers would have to rap on the counter to get her attention. By the time she was 12, it was as if she'd never been silent. Maya made up for her five years of semi muteness by gaining a reputation as precocious and eloquent.

One day Mrs. Flowers took Maya to the school library and told her to start reading, beginning with books starting with the letter A and continuing right through the alphabet. Maya indeed read every book in the library. She discovered the black poets Paul Laurence Dunbar, Langston Hughes, and James Weldon Johnson. She fell in love with Charles Dickens and William Shakespeare and Edgar Allan Poe.

"I was educated by those writers," Maya said. "Not about themselves and their people, but about me, what I could hope for."

When she graduated from grammar school with honors in 1940, she was probably the most well-read child in Stamps. And while finishing grammar school, which went through the eighth grade, marked the end of schooling for most black children, Maya was one of the few who would have a chance to go on to high school, but not in Stamps.

Angelou still doesn't know why Grandmother decided it was time for her and Bailey to go back to their mother. Most likely, she says, Grandmother knew that the children would always be at risk in the South. If they could finish their youth somewhere else, they should go. By this time, Vivian had settled in California, and at age 13, Maya returned to her mother.

Vivian played pinochle for money and ran a poker game. The lifestyle suited her; she loved the bars and the attention of the men. Soon after Maya and Bailey arrived, Vivian married the first man that Maya considered a father to her.

Daddy Clidell owned several apartment buildings and, later, pool halls. He was honest but not self-righteous. He taught Maya how to play poker and blackjack and how to avoid being a mark for con artists. Daddy Clidell moved the family to San Francisco, where they settled in the Fillmore district, San Francisco's Harlem.

Maya loved the city. School, however, was tough. She attended George Washington High School in a predominantly white section of town where for the first time, Maya was not considered brilliant. The other students spoke well and were often eager to participate in class discussions, while Maya cringed when a teacher called on her. Worse still, Maya was big for her age. At 13, she stood a self-conscious five feet nine inches. As Maya put it, she "felt like a horse."

Having received a scholarship to study dance after school at the California Labor School, Maya began to feel more at ease.

> My shyness at moving clad in black tights around a large empty room did not last long. Of course, at first, I thought everyone would be staring at my cucumber-shaped body with its knobs for knees, knobs for elbows and, alas, knobs for breasts. But they really did not notice me, and when the teacher floated across the floor and finished in an arabesque my fancy was taken. I would learn to move like that. I would learn to, in her words, "occupy space."

The summer of her 15th year, Bailey Sr. invited Maya to San Diego to spend the summer with him and his new girlfriend, Dolores Stockland. Dolores and Maya did not make fast friends.

During this visit, Bailey Sr. made frequent trips south of the border, supposedly to buy supplies for the Mexican dishes he cooked. He invited Maya along one day. They drove straight to a cantina in the mountains, where Bailey Sr. promptly got drunk and passed out. Maya managed to get him into the backseat of the car and, for the first time, she got behind the wheel and drove. She drove them down the mountain in the dark, hitting only one other car in the process.

When the two arrived home later that night, Dolores was a jealous wreck. She and Bailey Sr. argued well into the night with Bailey Sr. finally stomping out. Maya, feeling sorry for Dolores, went to comfort her. Dolores became enraged and stabbed Maya. When Bailey Sr. returned he took Maya to a friend to treat her wound. He then dropped her off at another friend's house to keep her apart from Dolores. He told her he'd be back for her the next afternoon.

Unable to bear staying in a stranger's house, Maya ran.

"I made a few tuna sandwiches, lumpy with pickles, put a Band-Aid supply in my pocket, counted my money (I had over three dollars plus some Mexican coins) and walked out," Maya said.

By evening she came to a junkyard and climbed into a gray sedan to spend the night. She awoke the following morning to find herself surrounded by the runaways who lived in the junkyard. The group of kids from white, black, and Mexican families took her in. They worked together, slept together, joked together; and even entered a dance contest together every weekend in an effort to snag the prize money. One night, Maya and a Mexican boy actually won second prize.

"The unquestioning acceptance by my peers had dislodged the familiar insecurity," Maya remembered. "Odd that the homeless children, the silt of war frenzy, could initiate me into the brotherhood of man. After hunting down unbroken bottles and selling them with a white girl from Missouri, a Mexican girl from Los Angeles and a black girl from Oklahoma, I was never again to sense myself so solidly outside the pale of the human race. The lack of criticism evidenced by our ad hoc community influenced me, and set a tone of tolerance for my life."

After a month, Maya was ready to go home. She phoned her mother, who sent her a plane ticket back to San Francisco, and Maya's days on the street ended.

Maya returned to a home at war. Bailey and Vivian were locked in a power struggle that ended with Vivian ordering him out of the house. At 16, Bailey left, holing up with a white prostitute he'd begun to pimp for. For Maya, the boy who had held her hand through so much childhood pain had disappeared. In search of a distraction, Maya decided the best way to forget his absence was to work—as a streetcar conductor, her perfect job. She imagined herself in the dark blue uniform with a money-changing belt around her hips, but when her mother informed her that black people weren't hired on the "cars," Maya became indignant: "Mother gave me her support with one of her usual terse asides: 'That's what you want to do? Then nothing beats a trial but a failure. Give it everything you've got. I've told you many times, can't-do is like don't-care. Neither of them [has] a home.'"

Maya's first visit to the Market Street Railway office was unsuccessful at securing her a position. Despite her quick dismissal on her first attempt, Maya would routinely return to the office over the course of several weeks. One afternoon, her perseverance paid off—the secretary who earlier dismissed her gave Maya the application forms. As Maya, who was then 15, put it, she "wove a cat's ladder of near truths and total lies," saying she was 19 and that she'd driven for a white lady in Stamps. She got the job.

Soon she was the first black woman to swing from the back of a trolley, collecting money and ushering riders into the car. She bought new clothes and opened a bank account. When she went back to high school for spring semester, Maya felt far more independent and sophisticated than her peers:

> They were concerned and excited over the approaching football games, but I had in my immediate past raced a car down a dark and foreign Mexican mountain. They concentrated great interest on who was worthy of being student body president, and when the metal bands would be removed from their teeth, while I remembered sleeping for a month in a wrecked automobile and conducting a streetcar in the uneven hours of the morning.

Feeling at odds with other girls her age, Maya began to question her sexuality, yet in her adolescent mind, she had always thought of lesbians as hermaphrodites. From her own perspective, her breasts were little more than flaps of skin, her torso didn't pinch in like a feminine hourglass, her feet and hands were mannishly large, and her voice was two notches too low.

"What I needed was a boyfriend," Maya thought. "A boyfriend would clarify my position to the world and, even more important, to myself."

At 16, Maya sought out a handsome and popular boy in the neighborhood and simply asked him if he'd like to have sex. He did. The act was quick and forgettable; she and the boy parted ways, casual and unconcerned. Three weeks later, Maya found herself pregnant.

Fearing her mother would make her drop out of high school, Maya hid her pregnancy. In May 1945, she graduated with the summer school class at San Francisco's Mission High School. That evening she told her mother and Daddy Clidell that she was more than eight months pregnant.

Vivian asked if she wanted to marry the father or if he wanted to marry her. Maya said no to both questions.

"Well, that's that," her mother said. "No use ruining three lives."

Shortly afterward, Maya gave birth to a son, Clyde Johnson.

"I had a baby," Angelou said. "He was beautiful and mine. Totally mine. No one had bought him for me. No one had helped me endure the sickly gray months."

With the war over and thousands of men returning home, it was not a good time for an unskilled black girl to find work. But Angelou now had a son to support and needed to make a decent wage. She applied for a job as a telephone operator, but was told she had failed their very basic IQ test. She eventually lied her way into a cooking job at a Creole restaurant and later moved on to a job as a cocktail waitress at the Hi Hat Club—often leaving Clyde in the care of her landlady.

Little Clyde was a year old now and Angelou found her way to mothering slowly, thinking little of leaving Clyde for long stretches of time. "He was my baby," she said, "rather like a pretty living doll that belonged to me. I was myself too young and unformed a human being to think of him as a human being."

The clientele at the Hi Hat often included prostitutes, con men, gamblers, thieves, and pimps. One night, two women who frequented the nightclub invited Angelou to their home for Sunday dinner. It was a strange night. Beatrice and Johnnie Mae were lesbians who prostituted themselves one night a week in order to pay for a little rented house in which they took great pride. The way Angelou viewed that evening, was that the two women were trying to seduce her.

Since Beatrice and Johnnie Mae's landlord had discovered their trade and wanted none of that in his place, Angelou offered to let the women rent the house in her name. She went further, offering to help the women find enough clients to work four nights a week. In return they would give her half their take.

As Angelou left their little house that evening she thought about what she'd just done. "In a successful attempt to thwart a seduction I had ended up with two whores and a whorehouse. And I was just 18."

Angelou came to the house each evening to pick up her cut and continued to work at the nightclub. She raked in the money, saving enough to pay cash for a new pale green Chrysler convertible. She was no longer the misplaced little girl; and was by contrast a quick-witted businesswoman.

"I had managed in a few tense years to become a snob on all levels—racial, cultural and intellectual," Angelou said. "I was a madam and thought myself morally superior to the whores. I was a waitress and believed myself cleverer than the customers I served. I was a lonely unmarried mother and held myself to be freer than the married women I met."

Before long Angelou and her two prostitutes had an argument and Beatrice and Johnnie Mae threatened to tell the police about what Angelou was doing. Terrified that the police would take Clyde if they found out, Angelou went home and packed. The next morning, she and Clyde were on a train heading back to Stamps.

Angelou felt safe and welcome in Stamps. Clyde cuddled into Annie's lap and Maya relaxed into the familiarity. To the black people of Stamps, Angelou was a celebrity. She had been to California and explored the big city. The warm embrace of the black community she had grown up in was just what she needed.

But Angelou found she didn't fit in there anymore. She had shrugged off the downcast eyes and humble speech that blacks in Southern towns wore like skin. One day she dressed in her best San Francisco shopping clothes and headed for a store in the white part of town. She and a white customer nearly bumped into each other in an aisle. As the salesgirl approached, the white woman jerked her head at Angelou and asked the salesgirl who this black woman was and where she was from:

"How do you pronounce your name, gal? Speak up."

In that moment I became rootless, nameless, pastless. The two white blurs buoyed before me.

"Speak up," she said. "What's your name?"

I clenched my reason and forced their faces into focus. "My name"—here I drew myself up through the unrevenged slavery—"is Miss Johnson. If you have occasion to use my name, which I seriously doubt, I advise you to address me as Miss Johnson. For if I need to allude to your pitiful selves, I shall call you Miss Idiot, Miss Stupid, Miss Fool or whatever name a luckless fate has dumped upon you.

"And where I'm from is no concern of yours, but rather where you're going. I'll slap you into the middle of next week if you even dare to open your mouths again."

On Angelou's return home, she found, Annie waiting on the porch, arms hanging at her sides. The news had already reached her. Angelou tried to explain, but Annie, who had never lifted her hand to Maya as a child, slapped her. Angelou sputtered on about principles but again and again, Annie slapped.

"You think 'cause you've been to California these crazy people won't kill you?" Annie said. "You think because of your all-fired principle some of the men won't feel like putting their white sheets on and riding over here to stir up trouble? You do, you're wrong. Ain't nothing to protect you and us except the good Lord and some miles."

To Dance

Angelou fled Stamps, heading back to her mother's home in San Francisco, and a job cooking at a greasy-spoon restaurant. Life was slipping away from her.

"I was nearly 19, had a baby, responsibilities and no real profession," Angelou recalled. "I could cook Creole and was a fast, friendly cocktail waitress. Also I was qualified as an absentee madam, but I somehow felt that I simply had not yet 'found out my niche.'"

As she contemplated her options, Angelou gave serious consideration to joining the army. Not only could she learn a trade and get college money through the G.I. Bill, but she could build a secure life for her son. In applying, she decided to try going straight to the top—Officer Candidate School.

Angelou passed the physical and psychological tests easily and was accepted. But just a week before she was to leave, the recruitment office withdrew their acceptance. They had discovered that the California Labor School, where Angelou had studied dance while she was in high school, was considered a communist organization.

Angelou was confused. She explained that she had no interest in communism, and virtually no interest in politics at all. But it was of little help; the army would not take her.

Deflated, Angelou settled into a job as a waitress and began smoking marijuana with abandon.

At that time, unbeknownst to Angelou, a tap dancer from Chicago named R. L. Poole was in town, looking for a dance partner. During his search, he came into contact with one of Angelou's friends, who had remembered that Angelou loved to dance. She kindly referred Angelou to Poole, and gave him Angelou's address.

When Poole showed up stating his intentions, Angelou quickly listed for him all of the popular dances she knew—the Texas Hop, the Off Time, the boogie-woogie, the Camel Walk—and, she added, she could do the splits. She proceeded to demonstrate leaping up and letting her legs slip to the floor. As she descended, her skirt seams gave way and one foot became caught between the legs of a nearby table while the other wedged itself behind the gas pipe. Hoping to prove she still possessed some grace, Angelou tried to free herself from the pipe, only to dislodge the pipe, sending gas hissing into the room.

Poole sprung up and shut off the gas, then lifted the table to free Angelou's other leg. Humiliated, she rolled over onto her stomach and cried. "There was no doubt that R. L. Poole had just witnessed his strangest audition," Angelou recalled. "The dark-brown face was somber and he said quietly, 'Well, anyway, you've got nice legs.'" She was hired.

Angelou threw herself into learning the steps for Poole's routine. At their first performance, she wore a red, white, and blue costume cut like a bathing suit. As she walked on stage at the small nightclub, she froze. Then she heard the music and "started dancing all over the place. Tapping, flashing, stashing up and down the floor." Poole had to drag her off stage.

"I loved it," Angelou remembered. "I was a hungry person invited to a welcome table for the first time in her life. . . . It was supercolossal. I had broken in. I was in show business. The only way was up."

Angelou quit her job as a waitress to practice full-time with Poole. While they danced at small clubs in the city, Angelou was sure Poole would be her ticket to Broadway.

As Angelou quickly learned, he wasn't. Poole's old girlfriend and dance partner returned and Poole dumped Angelou. Unemployed again, Angelou took the first job she could find. She returned to the kitchen as a fry cook in her mother's friend's restaurant in Stockton.

As she fried eggs and flipped burgers, Angelou fantasized of a better life. She dreamed about the man who would come to her rescue wearing conservative clothing and speaking softly. She dreamed of haveing a baby girl and living in a pretty house, where she would bake three-layer cakes and dote on her newfound man.

When Angelou met L. D. Tolbrook, she thought her fantasies had been realized. Tolbrook, a man of Angelou's father's age, wore tailor-made clothes and his nails were well manicured. Tolbrook began a carefully constructed seduction. As Angelou told him of her hardships he generously handed her money to help with Clyde.

His story to Angelou was that he was married to an older woman who was mean and ill—a woman to whom he felt a sense of duty. Angelou's heart went out to this patient, caring man, and soon they were making love. Angelou passion for Tolbrook consumed her blocking out everything but him.

As the relationship progressed, Tolbrook disclosed that he'd had some bad luck gambling. He had lost $5,000, and his debtors were trying to collect. "And I'm up to my neck," he told Angelou, "I was trying to win enough money . . . to divorce that old hag I'm married to and send her back to Louisiana. Then you and I could be together forever."

Tolbrook went on to say that he couldn't possibly ask for Angelou's help—he couldn't possibly ask her to sell her body to get him out of the jam.

To which Angelou responded, "L. D., if a woman loves a man, there is nothing too precious for her to sacrifice and nothing too much for him to ask."

With her consent, Tolbrook took Angelou to a brothel where she had expected to spend the next month trying to earn enough money in order to pay off Tolbrook's debt. During this time, Clyde would stay with his baby-sitter, Big Mary, and Angelou would see him on the days she had off.

Angelou never quite toke to prostitution. She kept trying to speak Spanish to her mostly Mexican customers, and within a week, she was the least popular woman in the house. Fortunately, her first week as a prostitute was also her last. During her first day off, Angelou learned that her mother, Vivian, had had a hysterectomy and needed her support back in San Francisco. She left Clyde at Big Mary's and went to visit with her mother.

While Vivian was recovering well, Maya discovered that her brother Bailey was facing his own difficulties. Bailey's wife, Eunice, had recently died after a long bout with pneumonia and tuberculosis, and Bailey had come unraveled.

Reuniting with her brother after their long time apart, Maya and Bailey spent hours talking and crying together. In catching up, Bailey told Maya all about Eunice and his life with her, while Maya, in turn, told him about Tolbrook and how she was helping him out.

Bailey saw through Tolbrook's scheme immediately. He ordered her to get Clyde and come home, insisting that Tolbrook was nothing more than a pimp.

While she refused to believe it, Angelou obeyed. She took a bus back to Los Angeles and went straight to Big Mary's. Upon arriving, she found the house boarded up. A neighbor informed her that Mary had moved three days earlier. Realizing that her son had been kidnapped, Angelou headed for Tolbrooks's house, sure that he would help her find Clyde. When Angelou told him what had happened, he called her a whore and told her to get lost. With her son missing, and Tolbrook's cold dismissal, Angelou's dream of a happy marriage and a cozy house seemed forever unattainable.

"I detested him for being a liar and a pimp, but more, I hated him for being such an idiot that he couldn't value my sterling attributes enough to keep me for himself alone," Angelou remembered. "There was no thought of the greed which coerced me to agree with L. D.'s plan in the hope that I'd win, in the end, a life of ease and romance."

Knowing that Big Mary had a brother in Bakersfield, Angelou caught a ride there that evening. As she arrived at his isolated farm, Angelou spotted movement from the driveway. Peering closely, she saw it was Clyde.

She swooped him up. He pushed away to see her face and started crying.

"I stood holding him while he raged about being abandoned," Angelou said. "My sobs broke free on waves of my first guilt. I had loved him and never considered that he was an entire person. . . . He was 3 and I was 19, and never again would I think of him as a beautiful appendage of myself."

Big Mary rushed out to explain herself. She had fallen in love with Clyde, and she begged Angelou to let her keep him. Angelou and Clyde fled for the bus station and a bus to San Francisco.

Angelou briefly took a job managing a restaurant in Oakland, after which she worked in a dress shop and real estate office. She was working so many hours that she had little time left for Clyde. On the eve of her day off each week, she would pick him up from the babysitter and he'd wrap himself around her and scream as they walked home. "When we were far enough away, he'd relax his stranglehold on my neck and I could put him down," Angelou said. "We'd spend the evening in my room. He followed my every turn and didn't trust me to go to the bathroom and return."

The guilt ate her raw. Angelou hoped for a job that would pay well enough to allow her to work fewer hours, yet she was suspicious when the white woman who owned the record store she frequented offered her a job. While Angelou had been taught never to trust a white person, she couldn't refuse the money, and she and Clyde moved back in with her mother.

Angelou enjoyed selling records, but she still dreamt of finding the man who would take care of her and Clyde. While at work, she made the acquaintance of a white sailor, who had dark hair and a face that reminded Angelou of Italian paintings. Tosh Angelos first inquired about a particular record, but his visits became more regular; before long, he was taking Maya and Clyde to parks to teach Clyde baseball.

When Tosh proposed, Maya answered yes, perhaps more in love with the idea of marriage than she was with Tosh. He was the first man to ask, and Maya would not refuse her dream. They married in the courthouse on a Monday morning, rented a large apartment, and Maya quit her job.

"I had a son, a father for him, a husband and a pretty home for us to live in," Maya said. "My life began to resemble a *Good Housekeeping* advertisement."

Tosh was kind, reliable, and intelligent. But after a year together, Maya saw the cracks that would break them apart. Not only did Tosh disapprove of Maya and Clyde spending time with their friends, but he had refused Maya her faith. She rebelled and began sneaking out to go to church at least one Sunday a month, careful to visit different churches so that no one would come to recognize her.

Then Maya began to notice the stares when she and Tosh were together.

"I stared back hard at whites in the street trying to scrape the look of effrontery off their cruel faces," Maya remembered. "But I dropped my eyes when we met Negroes. I couldn't explain to all of them that my husband [a Greek] had not been a part of our degradation. I fought against the guilt which was slipping into my closed life as insidiously as gas escaping into a sealed room."

After two and a half years, they divorced.

Free from domesticity, Angelou took off for New York after winning a scholarship to study dance with Pearl Primus, a choreographer whose creation of a group called Strange Fruit had won international acclaim. From there she went to Cleveland's Karamu House to teach dance. Her tenure there was short-lived—doomed by her inexperience and Afro hairstyle.

Angelou returned to San Francisco, still broke and still searching.

She found a sign outside a row of four seedy nightclubs: "Female Dancer Wanted. Good Take-Home Pay." At 24, Angelou was hired by one of them to dance six numbers a night for $75 a week in addition to working men for drinks in between. She'd get a quarter for each drink she got a man to buy her—with the "champagne" they would buy often being little more than clear soda. The B-girl work, as selling drinks was called, could earn her $10 a night.

Angelou quickly became the top drink seller. Rather than cajole and purr drinks out of customers, she beguiled them with honesty. She explained that for each drink they bought her, she got a cut. The more they bought, the longer she would chat with them. Angelou made good money this way, but it was her dancing that would change her world.

After two months at the Garden of Allah, people began coming just to watch Angelou move. One night she noticed a few couples in the audience who looked out of place. They were white, well dressed, and seemed cultured. "It occurred to me that they might be talent scouts and maybe I was going to be discovered," Angelou remembered. "I threw that silly thought out of my mind before it could take hold. Lana Turner and Rita Hayworth got discovered, black girls got uncovered."

It turned out the group was from the city's famed Purple Onion nightclub. Angelou's dancing impressed them and they began stopping by to watch her every evening. When the Purple Onion's lead singer left, the manager offered Angelou a six-month contract and set about turning her into a professional.

Not knowing how to write the music for the calypso songs she sang, Angelou found herself painfully ignorant. She couldn't even tell the piano player what key they were in. Choosing her stage name, however, was easy. Marguerite wouldn't do. The drama coach tried out over a dozen names before Angelou piped in: "My brother has always called me Maya." The drama coach liked that, but felt that Maya's married name of Angelos sounded too Spanish or Italian. So they changed the "s" to a "u," and she became Maya Angelou.

She wore long, snug dresses made out of raw silk, slit on both sides from floor to hip. Underneath she wore one-legged pants of bright batik. When she walked the dress opened, revealing one bare leg and one that appeared to be covered with tattoos. She would be barefoot—the Cuban queen.

"I counted three and walked slowly down the aisle and onto the stage," Maya said, remembering her first night. "I stood still as I had at rehearsal, and a dead calm surrounded me. One second later fear plummeted to my stomach and made my knees weak. . . .The aisle down which I had walked still lay open and unobstructed. I looked at it once, longingly, then turned to the pianist and nodded. And although I did not know it, another career for me had begun."

During the ensuing months, Angelou lived in a whirl of performances and publicity interviews. At times she forgot the music and would ask the audience to excuse her poor memory and bear with her dancing. She became known as much for her movements as her voice.

During her fourth month at the club, a touring show came to San Francisco. *Porgy and Bess* was an emotional and energetic folk opera about the lives of black people in South Carolina in the 1920s, performed by a black cast. Angelou was in awe. When producers of the show saw Angelou perform at the Onion, they too were in awe and asked her to audition. They offered her a role, but she had to decline because of the restrictions in the contract she had signed with the Onion. Angelou thought she'd lost her big chance. But two months later, just as her six-month Onion contract was expiring, she got another chance. *Porgy and Bess* was about to Europe and needed a singer for the role of Ruby. They wanted to know if Angelou would come?

"My mind turned over and over like a flipped coin," Angelou remembered. "Paris, then Clyde's motherless birthday party, Rome and my son's evening prayers said to Fluke, Madrid and Clyde struggling alone with his schoolwork.

"The past revisited. My mother had left me with my grandmother for years and I knew the pain of parting. My mother, like me, had had her motivations, her needs. I did not relish visiting the same anguish on my son. . . . But I had to work and I would be good. I would make it up to my son and one day would take him to all the places I was going to see.

NOTHING BEATS TRYING

Angelou sang and danced through Italy, France, Yugoslavia, Egypt, Athens, Israel, Spain, Morocco, and Switzerland. She sent half her wages home to her mother, who was watching Clyde. The managers had offered to let Angelou send for her son but she declined; she didn't want him exposed to the flamboyant homosexuals in the cast.

"Thus I had soothed my guilt, never admitting that I was reveling in the freedom from the constant nuisance of a small child's chatter," Angelou said. "I could send money home, write sad and somehow true letters reporting my loneliness and then stay up all night past daybreak partying with my friends."

Angelou was in Rome when she got a letter from her mother indicating that the family had fallen on hard times and Vivian planned to go to work as a card dealer in Las Vegas. Clyde, who had developed a severe rash that persisted despite treatment, needed his mother back. After almost two years on tour, Angelou returned to San Francisco and her son.

On her first night back, Clyde tiptoed into her room, his face puffy from tears. "He came to my bed and looked at me directly for the first time since my return," Angelou recalled. "He whispered, 'When are you going away again?'

"I put my arms around him and he fell sobbing on my chest. I held him, but not my own tears. 'I swear to you, I'll never leave you again. If I go, when I go, you'll go with me or I won't go.'"

Clyde's rash cleared as his fear diminished, and then one day, out of the blue, he announced that his name was no longer Clyde; he was Guy. It took a month to train the family, but soon they couldn't remember calling him anything else.

Angelou signed up with a local talent agency, adding to her application that she would only accept jobs that would accommodate Guy. She was surprised when an offer came from Hawaii. The Job paid $350 a week for four weeks of singing at a nightclub in Waikiki. The offer included transportation and accommodations for both her and Guy.

So Maya and Guy began life anew, Maya becoming a full-time mother for the first time. After Hawaii, she sang in clubs on the West Coast, with Guy by her side. They lived in a houseboat commune in Sausalito, a kind of

Bohemian life of bare feet, jeans, and radical white friends. The year was 1957 and America slow process of changing attitudes about race. Angelou was grateful that Guy was growing up around white people who "did not think of him as too exotic to need correction, nor so common as to be ignored."

While singing and walking barefoot, Angelou began to write—a few short stories and song lyrics. The first real writer she had shown her work to was John Killens, an author from New York who belonged to the famed Harlem Writers Guild.

"Most of your work needs polishing," he told Angelou. "In fact, most of everybody's work could stand rewriting. But you have undeniable talent." He encouraged Angelou to come to New York and join the guild, a group of writers who met in Killens's home to critique each other's work.

Like many before her, Angelou concluded that New York was the place to be for a young aspiring writer. She packed and soon found herself in the most literary city in the nation.

Angelou's first Harlem Writers Guild meeting was not a pleasant one. She read from a play she'd been working on called *One Love. One Life.* When she was finished, the first member/critic to comment said, "*One Life. One Love?*" His voice was carried an almost sarcastic kernel of disbelief. "I found no life and very little love in the play, from the opening of the act to its unfortunate end."

Angelou wilted. It seemed her writing career was over before it had begun. When the other writers broke for cocktails, Killens sidled up to her. "Good thing you stayed," he said. "You got some very important criticism. Don't just sit there. If they think you're too sensitive, you won't get such valuable criticism the next time you read."

What next time? Angelou wondered. Her writing was terrible. But as other writers chatted, Angelou began to understand. The purpose of the group was to rip the writing apart so that each author could reassemble the work in a better form.

"I sipped the cool wine and thought about the evening's instruction," Angelou remembered. "The writers assaulted my casual approach and made me confront my intention. If I wanted to write, I had to be willing to develop a kind of concentration found mostly in people awaiting execution. I had to learn technique and surrender my ignorance."

In order to pay the rent while she tackled the monumental task of becoming a passable writer, Angelou took a job singing at a club on the Lower East Side. Meanwhile, she began to awaken to a new interest in the events of her day. Angelou had never been particularly political, but her months in New York had exposed her to a new group of friends who talked about the events in Cuba, about Martin Luther King Jr., and about the struggle to end discrimination.

Shortly after being released from jail for civil disobedience, King traveled to New York on a fund-raising mission for the Southern Christian Leadership Conference, one of the organizations spearheading the growing civil rights movement. Angelou went to a church in Harlem to hear him speak.

" 'We, the black people, the most displaced, the poorest, the most maligned and scourged, we had the glorious task of reclaiming the soul and saving the honor of the country,'" Angelou remembered King saying.

King's words struck Angelou deeply. She and her then boyfriend sat by the Hudson River after King's speech, grasping for a way to help. They came up with Cabaret for Freedom, a revue to benefit the SCLC. They would produce the show, and find friends to act and sing in it.

Full of confidence, Angelou traipsed to the SCLC offices. After a shaky start, she convinced the office the revue was worth a try. Opening in the summer of 1960, Cabaret for Freedom was a hit. The crowded audience laughed at the comedy pieces, grew somber during the serious ones, and shot to their feet as the curtain closed.

On the heels of this success, Angelou learned that a short story she had written had been accepted by a magazine for publication. It didn't matter that the magazine was Cuban and printed only in Spanish; she had joined an elite group—published writers. The Harlem Writers Guild threw her a party.

The ego boost only grew when the SCLC offered her a job. They'd been impressed with how she managed Cabaret for Freedom and wanted her to run their New York office. She didn't know if she could do it, but typical to Angelou's style, she decided it was worth trying.

Angelou organized both black and white volunteers who stuffed envelopes, cleaned, and filed; she wrote letters and made telephone calls, all in hopes of raising money for King and his efforts. Blacks and whites worked together for change, protest marches and sit-ins abounded. It was a time of hope and action, and it thrilled 32 year-old Angelou.

Despite her previous experiences, Angelou hadn't given up on her hopes of finding a successful companion who could help take care of her. At one point, she had met a bail bondsman to whom she proposed, but in the midst of planning the wedding, Angelou met Vusumzi Make (often called Vus), a South African freedom fighter living in exile. He was in New York to petition the United Nations against South Africa's policies of racial apartheid. Angelou met him at John Killens's apartment, all the while; her friends and coworkers had been raging about this sharply intelligent man whose lectures were causing a stir. Angelou was surprised to meet a man who was both three inches shorter than she was, and had a baby face.

But when Make spoke about his work, Angelou was entranced.

"When he finished, he asked for questions and sat down, dabbing at his face with a cloud of white handkerchief," Angelou recalled. "My first reaction was to wish I could be the white cloth in his dark hand touching his forehead, digging softly in the corners of his lips. Intelligence always had a pornographic influence on me."

For the next two weeks, Make courted Angelou with flowers and conversation. He told her about his imprisonment in South Africa for political activities. He told her how the government had taken him into the desert and left him hundreds of miles from any town. He told her how he had eaten caterpillars, crawled over rocks, followed the stars, and walked out of South Africa to Ethiopia with one intention—to come to the United States and find a beautiful black woman who knew how to fight, a woman he would take back to Africa. Angelou was that woman.

Africa was adventure; Vus was purpose. Angelou said yes. She quit her job with the SCLC and prepared to leave with him for a conference in London. Make intended to marry her in England, but Angelou wanted to wait until they returned to New York so her family could attend. Make agreed to wait for a formal ceremony, but told Angelou he would privately marry her right then: "I am marrying you this minute," he said. "Will you say yes?" She said yes. "Then we are married." They never mentioned the word marriage again.

After London, Angelou set up house in New York. She became the consummate housewife. Vus handled the money while Maya decorated and cooked. While it appeared as if her fantasy had come to life, Angelou grew bored and uneasy.

She again threw her energies into activism. She had seen Malcolm X, the fiery leader of the Nation of Islam, speaking on a street corner one day and was drawn to his beliefs. He represented a new, more militant wing of activism that had grown tired of the nonviolent civil disobedience of King. He dismissed the help of white people, calling them devils and admonishing blacks not to trust them.

Angelou was taken by his speech. She had been growing frustrated with the lack of change in response to King's nonviolence and didn't agree with his philosophy that suffering was the foundation on which change would be built. She and several other women organized a protest at the United Nations, sparked by the death of a black freedom fighter in the Belgian Congo. The protest exploded into a riot, with Angelou taking to the streets along with hundreds of others.

Angelou and a friend later went to meet with Malcolm X to get his take on the riot and ask what they should do next. He rebuffed them by saying that the Nation of Islam did not protest nor did it try to gain freedom from whites; instead, they took freedom, and separated themselves from white society. Angelou thanked Malcolm X and left, disheartened and a little angry.

She again needed something more to hold her attention. At this time, a friend asked her to read a script from a play written by a French man, Jean Genet. *The Blacks* was a political play, arguing that oppressed people would eventually take over the crumbling society of the oppressors, but that they, in turn, would be no better. Angelou threw the script in the closet. Black people could never act like whites. She would never be part of such a play. But when she told Vus about the offer, he laughed, saying, "No wife of an African leader can go on stage."

While Angelou didn't like the play, she disliked her husband's attitude even more. She asked the play's producer to meet and talk to her husband, who came back from the meeting with the script and read all night.

> I was in a deep sleep when he shook me awake.
> "This play is great. If they still want you, you must do this play."
> I argued, "But the play says given the chance, black people will act as cruel as whites. I don't believe it."
> "Maya, that is a very real possibility. . . . You see, my dear wife, most black revolutionaries, most black radicals, most black activists, do not really want change. They want exchange. This play points to that likelihood. And our people need to face the temptation. You must act in *The Blacks*."

Angelou played the White Queen in the play's 1961 off-Broadway production.

"I started enjoying my role," Angelou said. "I used the White Queen to ridicule mean white women and brutal white men who had too often injured me and mine. Every inane posture and haughty attitude I had ever seen found its place in my White Queen."

As the play went on, Angelou marveled that three-fourths of the audience was invariably white. Why, she wondered, would white people come to hear insults spat at them by a black cast? One night she got her answer. A well-dressed white woman came to her crying after a performance. She'd seen the play five times:

> "Why? Why do you come back?" Angelou asked.
> "Well, well, we support you. I mean, we understand what you are saying."

"How many black friends do you have? I mean, not counting your maid?"

"Oh," she took a couple of steps backward. "You're trying to insult me."

I followed her. "You can accept the insults if I am a character on stage, but not in person, is that right?"

She looked at me with enough hate to shrivel my heart. I put my hand out.

"Don't touch me," the woman said.

She snatched her arm away, and spat out, "You people. You people." And walked away.

When a friend asked her what had happened, Angelou said, "She's one of our fans. She comes to the theater and allows us to curse and berate her, and that's her contribution to our struggle."

Meanwhile, Angelou began a very different struggle. She had been with Vus only a few months when she noticed the lipstick and perfume on his clothing. She washed out the foreign stains and smell and remained the dutiful wife. If he played a bit, if his body was unfaithful, she could close her eyes and pretend as long as his love was faithful.

It was the threats that she could not ignore. They began with a call at the theater. Angelou answered the phone, and a man's voice said, "Vusumzi will never come home again."

Was it a South African enemy? Was it a wronged husband? Angelou feared for her husband. When she told him, he explained that it was the South African police.

The calls became so frequent that Angelou began to think of the telephone as a "coiled cobra." One morning she received a call claiming Guy had been in a serious accident and was at the emergency room. She rushed to the hospital to find that Guy wasn't there, and was, instead, safe at school in history class.

In addition to the threats and infidelities, Angelou then learned that Vus had not been paying the rent. She came home to find an eviction notice on her door.

Vus told her not to worry, that not only did he have plenty of money, but it was time to move on to Egypt. Vus went ahead to get settled. When Maya and Guy boarded the plane for their new home, Maya felt the exhilaration of change. "Whether our new start was going to end in success or failure didn't cross my mind," she remembered. "What I did know, and know consciously, was that it was already exciting."

African Memories

Maya and Guy landed in Cairo to a different world.

"When we entered the center of Cairo, the avenues burst wide open with such a force of color, people, action, and smells, I was stripped of cool composure," Angelou remembered. Vus showed Maya and Guy into a luxurious home, complete with tapestries, French furniture, and brocade.

Her first few weeks in Cairo were a whirl of parties and introductions to freedom fighters from Uganda, Kenya, Tanganyika, North and South Rhodesia, Swaziland. She met diplomats and activists from all over Africa. Angelou entertained often, cooking gourmet meals for dozens of guests.

"I was a heroine in a novel teeming with bejeweled women, handsome men, intrigue, international spies and danger," Angelou said. "Opulent fabrics, exotic perfumes and the service of personal servants threatened to tear from my mind every memory of growing up in America as a second-class citizen."

Guy enrolled in high school, and he and Maya competed to learn Arabic. Before long, however, Angelou learned her opulent new life was all purchased on time. And Vus was once again behind on most of the payments.

With such a financially irresponsible husband, Angelou decided she needed a job. Through a friend she was offered a position as the associate editor of the *Arab Observer*, a local newspaper. Angelou accepted.

"You took a job without consulting me?" Vus fumed when she told him. "Are you a man?" He stalked the room, ranting about insolence, lack of respect, arrogance, defiance, callousness, lack of breeding. As his tirade went on, Angelou fell out of love.

"The last wisps of mystery had disappeared," she said. "There had been physical attraction so strong that at his approach, moisture collected at every place where my body touched itself. Now he was in hand's reach, and tantalization was gone. He was just a fat man, standing over me, scolding."

Angelou didn't know much about journalism. She had exaggerated her writing experience to get the job. Now she was faced with handling 12 reporters, covering African politics, learning a new jargon, and filling a weekly paper. She read everything she could find about running a newspaper.

At first she took news releases from the Telex machine, added background information, wrote new headlines, and put her byline on the stories. In the year she worked at the *Observer*, she learned how to find and report her own stories; how to write with just enough persuasion to leave readers thinking an idea had been their own. She also learned the political landscape of the newly independent African nations. Along the way she began writing commentary for Radio Egypt. And while Angelou worked, Vus continued with his extramarital activities. Angelou let it go, again. Until one night he tried to take his infidelities one step further. Vus informed Angelou that he was thinking of taking a second wife, as African custom allowed.

"At that second, I hardened my heart," Angelou remembered. "I didn't believe all the legitimizing drivel Vus concocted about African male infidelity and I would not allow him to teach such nonsense to my son."

Angelou told Vus she'd be leaving him. Guy would soon be graduating from high school and Maya wanted him to enroll at the University of Ghana, known to be the best in Africa. A friend helped Angelou get a job at the Liberian Department of Information, and she told Vus goodbye.

"Vus accepted my departure with undisguised relief," Angelou said. "We had worn our marriage threadbare, and it was time to discard it." In 1962, Maya and Guy boarded a plane bound for West Africa, for what Angelou thought of as the real Africa.

The plane landed in Accra, Ghana's capital, where Maya planned to settle Guy into college before heading to Liberia for her new job. While staying with Vus's friends, Guy was invited to a picnic, and Maya began to organize his clothing. When the doorbell rang Angelou knew something was wrong—Guy had been in an accident. Maya rushed to the hospital where she found Guy unconscious but breathing. A truck had hit the car he was driving. X-rays determined that his arm and leg were fractured and his neck had been broken in three places.

"The crash, my pale son, his awful clammy skin, my love for him, all rushed into my brain at once," Angelou remembered. She functioned in a daze through Guy's move to a military hospital, where he'd get better treatment.

Guy would remain in the hospital for a month, after which he needed at least three months at home to mend. Angelou canceled her plans to work in Liberia, rented a room at the YWCA, and again looked for a job. Through her friends she found an administrative assistant job at the School of Music and Drama at the University of Ghana's Institute of African Studies. She and Guy moved into the house of a traveling instructor. Still shrouded around his head, neck, and shoulders by a hard cast, Guy took the university's entrance exam and was accepted. The day Maya helped Guy move into his dorm room was the first day of a new life for Maya.

"I closed the door and held my breath," Angelou said, "waiting for the wave of emotion to surge over me, knock me down, take my breath away. Nothing happened. I didn't feel bereft or desolate. I didn't feel lonely or abandoned. . . . I sat down, still waiting. The first thought that came to me, perfectly formed and promising, was 'At last, I'll be able to eat the whole breast of roast chicken by myself.'"

Angelou loved Ghana. It was less segregated, and for the first time in her life she didn't have to fight anybody. Angelou had grown accustomed to spending a third of her energy just fighting the racism around her.

> Well, of course, everybody around me was black, so for the first time in my life, my defenses not only did not work, they were not necessary, not those particular ones. . . . Then I began to examine my people and I thought, my God! How did we survive this! Good Lord! It's like growing up with a terrible sound in your ears day and night. Terrible, a kind of sound that is unrelenting, that pulls your hairs up on your body. And then to be away from it. At first you miss it, naturally, but then when you get used to the peace, the quietude, the lack of pressure. . . .

Angelou made new friends. She laughed often, argued politics, and spoke Fanti so well she was often mistaken for a tribal native. She learned to cook with lamb, curry, pineapples, tomatoes, papaya, and mangos.

Angelou spent three years in Ghana, from 1963 to 1966, leaving only to tour with the reunited cast of *The Blacks* for performances in Berlin and Venice. She wrote freelance for the *Ghanaian Times*, and worked as a liaison between the government and American expatriates there. She also worked for the Ghanaian Broadcast Corporation, edited features for the *African Review*, and played the lead role in *Mother Courage* at the university.

Angelou had long mourned what she imagined was black Americans' loss of their African heritage—the traditions and views that make a people unique. But traveling throughout Ghana, Angelou saw that much of Africa was still present in American blacks. She saw that American blacks, much like those in Ghana, still called each other by familiar names—uncle, cousin, brother, sister. In Ghana's small towns, where hotels were sparse, families invited travelers into their homes for the night, while friends and neighbors discreetly brought food to feed the unexpected guests—a custom Angelou had witnessed in Stamps.

"I used to say on soap boxes in Harlem that slavery removed, stole our culture," Angelou recalled. "But that's baloney. And I had to admit, I had to say, 'Look, I was wrong.'"

Angelou, like many of the black Americans who journeyed to Africa, searched for her roots. She visited Cape Coast and Elmina castles, which were holding forts for captured slaves. She felt the echoing cries hundreds of years old, and she watched the native people and places. Angelou remembered:

I loved to imagine a long-dead relative trading in those marketplaces, fishing from that active sea and living in those exotic towns, but the old anguish would not let me remain beguiled. Unbidden would come the painful reminder—'Not all slaves were stolen, nor were all slave dealers European.' . . . Were those laughing people who moved in the streets with such equanimity today descendants of slave-trading families? Did that one's ancestor sell mine or did that grandmother's grandmother grow fat on the sale of my grandmother's grandmother?

Angelou was usually friendly and eager to befriend Africans. As a liaison between the Ghanaian government and American blacks, she was able to meet many of the important black activists and thinkers traveling to Ghana.

In 1965, Angelou and several friends organized a march in Ghana to coincide with King's March on Washington. Although Angelou was no longer taken with King's nonviolent civil disobedience tactics, she felt a show of solidarity was important. A crowd met at midnight with placards and torches to march to the American Embassy.

Shortly after the march, Malcolm X arrived in Accra after a trip to Mecca. Angelou joined others at a friend's house to listen to him. She found a man much changed since her brief meeting with him in New York. "He said that though his basic premise that the United States was a racist country held true, he no longer believed that all whites were devils, nor that any human being was inherently cruel at birth," Angelou remembered.

He knew his followers would not like the change in his philosophy, and he severed his ties with the Nation of Islam in 1964. Still, Angelou admired Malcolm X and listened closely to his words as she drove him to various functions and meetings, often sitting in on discussions.

Several months later, Malcolm X, who was back in the United States and who had been corresponding with Angelou and her friends, wrote that the organization he had set up after his break with the Nation of Islam, the Organization of Afro-American Unity, needed someone to coordinate and run its offices. Although he didn't ask Angelou specifically, she felt called. Guy wanted to stay at the university, but Angelou knew it was time. At 38, she returned to California:

If the heart of Africa still remained elusive, my search for it had brought me closer to understanding myself and other human beings. Many years earlier I, or rather someone very like me and certainly related to me, had been taken from Africa by force. This second leave-taking would not be so onerous, for now I knew my people had never completely left Africa. . .it was Africa which rode in the bulges of our high calves, shook in our protruding behinds and crackled in our wide open laughter.

LISTENING FOR THE RHYTHM

Angelou arrived back in San Francisco in February of 1965 eager to begin working with Malcolm X. She'd been home only three days when a friend called to say that Malcolm X had been assassinated, allegedly by Black Muslims (followers of the Nation of Islam) angry at his softening views. Angelou was stunned; she'd just talked to him on the phone the day before. He'd told her he was being threatened and had had a close call in New York, where a white man had rescued him when someone tried to shoot him. How could she have thought of coming back to a country, Angelou wondered, where such a great leader could be dismissed with a bullet?

At that instant, Angelou decided to turn away from activism, at least as a direct supporter, and would focus instead on writing; her first projects were for the stage. In 1966, her two-act play, *The Least of These*, was staged in Los Angeles. Two other plays she wrote that year were never produced. She also went back to acting, appearing in a modern version of the play *Medea*, the story of a woman who murders her children.

But Angelou couldn't stay away from the cause for long. She ran into King at a tribute at Carnegie Hall, where he asked her to work for him to raise support from the nation's black preachers for his coming march against poverty. He needed her for only a month, and Angelou agreed.

On April 4, 1968, as Angelou was cooking for a party, a friend asked if she had listened to the radio: King had just been killed in Memphis.

The murders of Malcolm X and Martin Luther King deeply affected Angelou. She had known so many civil rights workers who had been killed or imprisoned. The riots in Los Angeles, Detroit, Baltimore, and elsewhere that erupted after King's death left Angelou grasping with unanswered questions. What would happen to the movement now? What kind of country would do this to its heroes?

It was a tragic year for Angelou but also one that marked her maturation as a writer. She directed a play, *Moon on Rainbow*, and wrote a 10-part series for National Educational Television about African traditions in American life called *Black! Blues! Black!*. She also recorded several of her poems on an album, *The Poetry of Maya Angelou*.

Despite the growing acclaim she received as a writer and actress, part of Angelou was still the misplaced girl who dreamed of a man to adore. There had been too many men with too little of what she needed. Angelou, at 41, had grown desperate.

One afternoon, after having just been named the *New York Post*'s Person of the Week, Angelou walked into her favorite New York bar, Terry's Pub, and found herself the toast of the town. Journalists, actors, musicians, professors, models, and writers gathered around her, shouting congratulations. The bartender offered her a huge martini.

"Eventually the toasters returned to their tables and I was left to grow gloomy in silence," Angelou remembered. "Moodiness and a creeping drunkenness from too many martinis dimmed the room and my spirits."
As she drank her martinis, she watched a table of five young black journalists enjoying themselves. The men had been part of the cadre of well-wishers but had retreated to themselves.

"A tear slipped down my cheek," Angelou remembered. "I gathered my purse and, removing myself from the stool, gingerly pointed myself in the direction of the journalists' table." She pulled up a chair and launched into a litany of her attributes—housekeeping, cooking, writing, dancing, languages, and lovemaking. Why, she demanded, with all these qualities, did none of them find her alluring? Why was she alone?

"In one second I realized that I had done just what they feared of me," Angelou said. "That I had overstepped the unwritten rules which I knew I should have respected. Instead, I had brazenly and boldly come to their table and spoken out on, of all things, loneliness."

Angelou began to cry. When she sobered up at home that night, she thought back on her romances. After Tosh she had consciously chosen lovers only from among black men. Perhaps she had narrowed the field too far. Angelou decided to no longer let race influence her in choice of companions.

Angelou had become friends with James Baldwin, a famous black author who one evening he took her to a dinner party at the home of cartoonist Jules Feiffer and his wife Judy. They drank scotch and talked until 3 A.M. Angelou's stories of her life, from Stamps to Ghana, captured her hosts. The next morning Judy called Robert Loomis, a friend at Random House, and encouraged him to get Angelou to write her autobiography.

Loomis called Angelou, who was living in New York while producing a television series on the West Coast—she said no. He persisted, and during the third call, when Angelou turned him down again, he said it was probably for the best, because autobiographies are the most difficult form of writing.

That challenge was all it took. Angelou, 42, did an about-face and said she'd do it. She went to London to write, dredging the past "from the tunnel of memory."

I Know Why the Caged Bird Sings covered Angelou's life from her early years in Stamps to the birth of her son. She dedicated it to Guy and "all the strong black birds of promise who defy the odds and gods and sing their songs." When the book was published in 1970, it made the nonfiction best-seller list within a week. Angelou was the first black woman to accomplish that feat. Soon the book was nominated for a National Book Award and became required reading on college campuses across the nation.

With *Caged Bird*, Angelou established a public reputation that still defines her today—that of a survivor. She wrote frankly about the tragedy in her life—the abandonment, the rape, the muteness. To her readers she became a victim who had fought, survived, and excelled.

With a best-selling book on the shelves, Angelou was flooded with offers to speak at universities across the country, but she steadfastly refused those from Southern schools. Even the sound of a Southern accent would fill Maya with surges of hate and urges to scream. The South had become an obsession, a place on which to fasten all her anger and fear about racism. As she came to understand how this obsession was hurting her, both in lost speaking fees and in the fears she hadn't confronted, she decided to face the South again. She accepted her first southern speaking offer from Wake Forest University in North Carolina. She was so nervous about the lecture that she almost canceled it. In an attempt to overcome her nervousness, she convinced a friend to join her, and the two of them headed south to North Carolina.

"I walked to the podium, and looked out into a filled and racially mixed auditorium," Angelou remembered. "Prohibitions against integration had long since been removed legally in the South, but I had never actually imaged whites and blacks sitting together in a Southern state. Understandably, I was taken aback."

When Angelou finished her lecture on African traditions still prevalent in America, the audience stood to applaud. "If I was thrown before, now I was dumbfounded," she later recalled. "I had pulled no punches, and softened no points, yet Whites stood beside Blacks, clapping their hands and smiling."

At the end of an impromptu question-and-answer session, a university official offered Angelou a place at Wake Forest if she ever wanted to try teaching, and two white women invited her home for drinks. Angelou got back to her hotel room at 3 A.M. thinking the South had changed.

Contrary to her experiences the night before, Angelou and her friend went out the next morning for a good Southern breakfast with grits and biscuits, where the white waitress took their order and then ignored them for 20 minutes. "At last, the South I knew had emerged," Angelou recalled. "At last, the insult and humiliation which I had dreaded were to be placed on my head." Angelou warned her friend that she was not going to tolerate this; she intended to make a scene.

Angelou clapped her hands and ordered the waitress over. "We ordered 20 minutes ago. Where is the food? Or don't you serve black people?"

The waitress shook her head. "No, ma'am," she said. "It ain't that. It just we run out of grits. We can't serve no breakfast 'til the grits is done."

Angelou laughed, her outrage melting. The South had changed. The South's hold on Angelou relaxed, and she began to think more kindly of this place that held so much of her own childhood memories and the memories of black Americans.

In the midst of her lecturing travels, Angelou accepted an offer from Columbia Pictures to write a script based on Alex Haley's book *Autobiography of Malcolm X*. She was the fourth writer to attempt the script, and her work, like those before her, was dismissed. However, other writing opportunities would come.

Since her years in Stamps, when Mrs. Flowers initiated her into the world of verse, Angelou had been writing poetry, and in 1971, she published her first book of poetry, *Just Give Me a Cool Drink of Water 'Fore I Diiie*. The book was nominated for a Pulitzer Prize

This success afforded Angelou the opportunity to try something new— an original screenplay. Ever since her experience in Terry's Pub, Angelou had been thinking about the relationship between black men and black women. It was a relationship that had repeatedly failed her, and she felt writing about it would help her to learn why. In the story, her main character, Georgia, has just become a singing celebrity in Sweden. However, despite her fame, she is still a lonely woman, unable to find a black man to be her partner. After taking up with a white photographer, she is strangled by a racist zealot.

The movie was filmed in Sweden and Angelou traveled there to oversee the production. When *Georgia, Georgia* was released in 1972, Angelou became the first black woman to have an original screenplay produced. She was also thrown into a den of criticism. Her women friends called to thank her for vindicating them onscreen, while her black male friends complained they didn't deserve such a negative portrayal. Angelou held steady. She said that both black men and women deserve the blame for their crumbling relationships. But she was a woman and this was her side of the story: In her experience, Angelou had not been able to form a meaningful, long-term relationship with a black man despite her desire, her longing, and her active searching since adolescence.

After Sweden, Angelou settled in Berkeley, California, to work on a screenplay for *Caged Bird*. She finished the script, but disagreements over choosing a director shelved the project. It would not be produced for several years and then only as a made-for-television movie. Angelou continued to work in television, narrating and hosting several specials about African-American life.

By the age of 44, Angelou had been a professional actress, singer, dancer, journalist, autobiographer, screenwriter, and poet. When an interviewer asked her where she found the energy and time to tackle so many different forms of art, Angelou explained that not having a man helped: "I have the energy, and more importantly, I have lots of time. My looks don't fit the current fashion in terms of feminine beauty. I am a woman who is black and lonely."

Focus also helped. Angelou worked on one project at a time, often consumed by her characters: "It's as if I've been created by my characters just to draw them," she explained. "I'm not fit company for man or beast."

With each new project, Angelou would first write down everything she knew about the subject, maybe 12 or 14 pages. Over the next few days, she would read her notes, searching for the subject's rhythm, and then she would weed until she found the salient points. With this, the work would take shape. "And then I try to enchant myself into that particular situation I want to write about, just cover myself in it, and keep listening for the rhythm," she explained.

When she wrote, Angelou unplugged the phone, closed drapes, told her friends not to bother her, and worked 16 hours a day. She may have taken breaks to walk, garden, or clean the house, but that was it. During one marathon writing session, she heard someone knocking on the door and just ignored it. The knock persisted, and Angelou finally opened the door to find a friend with a casserole. The friend handed the casserole to her, turned around, and left. "I took it, and then I realized that for the past four or five days I'd just been drinking Scotch and eating cheese and bread—that's all there was in the fridge."

WRESTLING DEMONS

By the early 1970s, the feminist movement was in high swing and Angelou, as a strong, public woman, was often asked to lend her voice to the cause. She did so willingly, believing in equal pay, respect, and responsibility, but she began to see that gender relations for white women were different than those for black women.

It seemed that most feminists were affluent white women who had time to be introspective about their gender's place in the world, while most black women were working two jobs to feed their kids. Moreover, black women had more power in relation to black men than white women had with white men. As Angelou had seen it, many feminists had lost their sense of humor. By the mid-1980s Angelou would remove herself from most feminist organizations that weren't specifically for black women and begin referring to herself as a "womanist."

Angelou was also less idealistic about women then many feminists. Angelou recalls a party in London in the early 1970s, in which a woman with an affected British accent was chatting with her and a few others:

> "If women ruled the world," she said, "we wouldn't have had the cruelties, the famines, the wars." Then she turned to me where I was standing drinking and she asked, "Don't you agree, my dear?"
>
> I looked at her and said, "Not at all, my dear. I don't agree. I remember the Medicis. Oh, no. I remember the empress of China. I remember the women who spat on the little black children who were trying to go to school. And I know that somebody washes the sheets for the Ku Klux Klan. Do you think those macho men wash their own sheets? Make no mistake. Women do it." And I said, "Anyway, I don't come to cocktail parties to speak about issues of such pith and moment. I come to drink. So excuse me."

Angelou walked away from the conversation and into her next love affair. Paul Du Feu had noticed her mingling at the party and invited her to dinner.

Du Feu was younger than Angelou, white, handsome, and British. He was a writer and cartoonist who had been married to feminist writer Germaine Greer. Angelou and Du Feu fell in love and were married in 1973 at the multiracial Glide Community Church in San Francisco. Angelou was 45.

Maya and Paul wanted to live in the wine country and settled in California's Sonoma Valley. Du Feu was skilled at refurbishing old houses, and the couple found a rambling ranch house on two acres filled with Japanese gardens, a pond with carp, and a bridge. A huge pool lay on the hilly land. Angelou settled in to gourmet cooking, vegetable gardening, and decorating the walls with African masks and drawings of black women and children. Her son Guy, who had also returned to the San Francisco area, had a son of his own, Colin Ashanit Murphy-Johnson, and Maya relished her role as grandmother.

Angelou described those times with Du Feu as gloriously happy. They respected each other, had great healthy arguments, and learned from each other's differences.

Du Feu encouraged Angelou's writing like no other man had. He had written his own book, *Let's Hear It for the Long-Legged Woman*, and he prompted Angelou to be more open—to lay more of herself bare before her readers.

After her first book, people often asked Angelou how she had escaped a poor, broken home and overcome the many trials she had faced in her life. "How the hell do you know I did escape?" Angelou would often answer. "You don't know what demons I wrestle with." Her second autobiography would reveal those demons.

In *Gather Together in My Name*, Angelou showed readers that she didn't escape—that her life became a series of painful falls and desperate attempts to find love and acceptance. It was the small miracles that sustained her, the love of her brother and mother, the kindness of friends.

While working on her book, she began an odd but effective writing routine that has remained her preferred work environment. Each morning she wakes at 5:30, showers and drives to a hotel room she keeps just for writing. The maids have been instructed to remove all the pictures from the room. By 6:30 she settles in with just a Bible, thesaurus, dictionary, yellow legal pads, cigarettes, playing cards, crossword puzzles, and a bottle of sherry.

That room is sacred. "When I approach the door, it is with utter apprehension and anticipation," Angelou says. "It is frightening. It is what I am."

She props herself up in bed, and begins. "I write on the bed lying down—one elbow is darker than the other, really black from leaning on it— and I write in longhand on yellow pads. Once I'm into it, all disbelief is suspended; it's beautiful. I hate to go."

By two or three o'clock in the afternoon, she packs up her things and returns home. In the evening she often edits, whittling 10 or 12 pages down to 3 or 4. And the process continues the next day.

Writing is Angelou's life and she has not taken it lightly since her first evening at the Harlem Writers Guild. But in the 1970s, she dabbled, like she always had, in many other artistic endeavors as well. In 1973 Angelou played Mary Todd Lincoln's dressmaker in the Broadway production of *Look Away*, a two-character play that closed after one performance. She also wrote another screenplay, *All Day Long*. For television, Angelou wrote two specials about black American culture—"The Legacy" and "The Inheritors"—and played the wife of a drunken Richard Pryor on an NBC special for which she also wrote a segment. In 1979, *Caged Bird* made it to production as a CBS special.

She wrote a second book of poetry, *Oh Pray My Wings Are Gonna Fit Me Well*, which came out in 1975. In 1976, her third autobiography, *Singin' and Swingin' and Gettin' Merry Like Christmas* came out, covering Angelou's life from a San Francisco record store through her European tour with *Porgy and Bess*. In 1978, Angelou's third book of poetry, *And Still I Rise*, came out. Some of the poems in the book were set to music and choreographed into a dance program that opened in Washington D.C. and later on Broadway.

Between such endeavors she has taught classes at several universities as a visiting instructor and garnered many awards. In 1975, President Gerald Ford appointed Angelou to the American Revolution Bicentennial Council, and she received her first honorary doctorate, from Smith and Mills College. Twenty-five years later, Angelou would have 50 such honorary titles.

In 1976, *Ladies Home Journal* named her as the Woman of the Year in Communications, and in 1977, President Jimmy Carter named Angelou to the National Commission on the Observance of International Women's Year. In that same year, her PBS documentary *Afro-Americans in the Arts* won a Golden Eagle Award.

She was later nominated for an Emmy Award for her acting in the seminal television miniseries *Roots*. She played Kunta Kinte's grandmother, Nyo Boto. While her name had been known for years, *Roots* made her face just as recognizable.

"I found that people knew me," Angelou said. "I walked down the street, especially the first month [of the TV series]. I've written five books, I can't say how many plays, movie scripts, music, and poetry, and so forth. I walk down the street and people say, 'You're that actress in *Roots*. What's your name again, and what have you been doing all this time?'"

The success and fame was partly to blame, Angelou has said, for her deteriorating relationship with Du Feu, who couldn't handle the demands of celebrity. Angelou has also blamed their house, claiming that it was jinxed—bread wouldn't bake and chicken wouldn't fry. "We were a rather eccentric, loving, unusual couple determined to live life with flair and laughter," Angelou said. "It was a great marriage, though we wore it out; we just used it up."

After their separation, Angelou felt that she couldn't stay in California. She didn't want to run into Du Feu or the next woman he might find. In 1981, she moved to Winston-Salem. The town had welcomed her years before and begun softening her attitudes toward the South. So when Wake Forest University offered her a teaching position, Angelou was ready to return. She bought a 10-room brick colonial house, which she later expanded to 18 rooms, and settled in alone.

After her soured marriage to Du Feu, Angelou stopped being as candid about her relationships with men. In several interviews, she refused talk about how many times she'd been married. Maya explained:

> The reason is that the number would make me appear to be frivolous. But in each marriage I brought all of myself and put in all my energy and loyalty, excitement, fidelity and hard work. The only thing is, when a marriage doesn't work I am one to say, "Hey, I'm unhappy, and it's not given to me to live a long time." So I've left a number of men, but I've been loved a great deal and have loved a great deal.

Part of the trouble, Angelou has said, has been race. She married two white men and says racial history always came into play. Even an argument over picking up socks felt ripe with racial overtones.

"I've married white men. I've married black men, Africans," Angelou has said. "I've never married an American white. That's not to say that I won't tomorrow. But I hope that the next man who takes my fancy will be a black American—just for life to be simpler. I adore black men."

But Angelou would soon give up on finding her man. She said she couldn't picture herself marrying again and felt that a partner would diminish her. "Being strong and daring doesn't mean you don't cry yourself to sleep at night," Angelou said. "But if I had to give up a quarter of my devotion and excitement for a man . . . well, I cannot do it."

Alone in her new home, Angelou set about creating a life all her own. In 1981, she told another chapter of that life in her fourth autobiography, *The Heart of a Woman*, covering the years she spent in Africa.

Angelou is one of the few modern writers to choose autobiography as her primary form of expression, to choose her own life as the vehicle for her literary exploration. Writing about herself is a strange sort of exercise. At once she must delve into her psyche, yet create a distance from herself, a character of herself. The point of her autobiographies, Angelou claims, is not just for the reader to learn about Maya Angelou:

> I use the first person singular and I'm talking about the third person plural all the time; what it's like to be a human being. So the person who reads my work and suspects that he or she knows me, hasn't gotten the half of the book, because he or she should know himself or herself better after reading my work. That's my prayer.

Angelou writes with such immediacy and seemingly effortless power that critics sometimes refer to her as a natural writer, which infuriates her."That sometimes will make me so angry that I will cry, really, because my intent is to write so it seems to flow," she says. "Sometimes I will stay up in my room for a day trying to get two sentences that will flow, that will just seem as if they were always there."

Between writing projects, Angelou continued working for television. She wrote the pilot episode of a proposed NBC series *Sister, Sister*, which aired in 1982 but never became a series. For public television she narrated a special, "Humanities Through the Arts."

Shortly before moving to North Carolina in 1982, Angelou was forced to revisit one of the terrifying moments of her past when her grandson, Colin, was kidnapped. One day Guy had gone to pick Colin up from a visitation with his mother. The house was empty and she and Colin were gone.

Guy and his ex-wife had a custody arrangement in which Colin spent a weekend with her every month. For Colin's mother, however, it wasn't enough as she began what would be a four-year stint of running and hiding to keep her son. Angelou felt the same lurch of impossibility she had felt 40 years before when Guy's baby-sitter had kidnapped him.

After several months, Angelou moved to North Carolina, knowing there was nothing more she could do. While she and Guy waited, Guy was diagnosed with a growth on his spinal column in his neck. He would have to undergo a risky surgery that could leave him paralyzed or even dead.

"If I don't survive, find my son," he told his mother at the hospital just before the surgery. "Explain how much I loved him. Teach him, as you taught me, to laugh. Teach him discipline. Teach him to love learning. Above all, Mom, teach him to love."

After surgery, Guy was unable to move for several weeks. At this point, Angelou took control of the effort to find Colin. She hired a battery of private detectives but no one could find her grandson. When seven months after his surgery Guy was walking again, although with difficulty, the two of them combined their efforts to find Colin. Angelou even added a bedroom for Colin at her house and decorated it just for him, in red and blue.

In May of 1985, Angelou finally got the call she had been waiting four years for. A friend of Colin's mother knew where she was and had decided to tell Angelou. Within a week Colin was in Angelou's arms, yelling, "Grandma, Grandma."

"I reached inside myself all the way back to my own grandmother and found enough reserve to keep from screaming (I didn't want to frighten the boy)," Angelou recalled. "I took him in my arms and said, 'What a wonderful fellow you are, and I am so happy to touch you again.'"

With her grandson's return, Angelou's small family was complete again.

Shortly after moving to North Carolina, Wake Forest University expanded its offer to Angelou with a lifetime appointment to the Reynolds chair as Professor of American Studies. The appointment caused a stir. While most professors were only offered such positions for two to five years, Angelou had it for life. She would be asked to teach only one semester a year, giving her the spring and summer to write. She used the time to create another volume of poetry, *Shaker, Why Don't You Sing*, published in 1983.

In 1984, the governor of North Carolina appointed Angelou to the board of the North Carolina Arts Council. She had become known as a Renaissance woman, with her forays into such diverse kinds of art.

In 1985, she wrote a play entitled *The Southern Journey*, and in 1986, she published her fifth autobiography, *All God's Children Need Traveling Shoes*. She also produced a CBS program about teenage boys as parents. In 1987 she published another book of poetry, *Now Sheba Sings the Song*, about the strength and beauty of black women, and she wrote lyrics for an album recorded by Roberta Flack.

Living on her own, Angelou's life settled into a quiet routine—checking paperwork with her secretary, straightening before the housekeeper arrives, and entertaining friends. When writing, however, she would be at her stark hotel room by 7 A.M., home by early afternoon, and editing late into the night. This schedule continues today.

GOIN' ON

In the 1990s, Angelou made a point of being available to lend her presence and words to people and causes in which she believed:

> I make myself available to black politicians because I know that if these two powers are linked something wonderful happens. If a person is running for office and I come and recite *And Still I Rise* or *Phenomenal Woman*, it just adds to her power. The one hand trying to wash itself is a pitiful spectacle, but when one hand washes the other, power is increased, and it becomes a force to be reckoned with.

In the early 90s, Angelou would add her power and poetry to several illustrious institutions. In November of 1992, Angelou took a phone call from a man on President-elect Bill Clinton's Inaugural Committee. Clinton, who had grown up in Hope, Arkansas, just 25 miles from Stamps, felt a kind of kinship with Angelou, and he wanted her to write a poem for his inauguration ceremony. Angelou was stunned. The last poet to read at an inauguration was Robert Frost at John F. Kennedy's 1961 celebration. Furthermore, no black poet had ever done so.

"I didn't take it all in at the time," Angelou remembered. "I was bowled over. I did sit down."

News of Angelou's invitation spread quickly. In the weeks before the January event, Angelou received hundreds of letters and calls from people offering both congratulations and ideas for the poem. Black people often said they wanted her to tell their story. White people often said they wanted her to speak against racial division.

"The writing of poetry is so private, so reclusive, one has to really withdraw inside one's self to a place that is inviolate," Angelou said. "But when a whole country knows that you are writing a poem, it is very hard to withdraw. Even on an airplane, people would pass by my seat and say, 'Mornin', finish your poem yet?'"

Angelou went back through some of her favorite writers—W. E. B. Du Bois, Frederick Douglass, and several black preachers. She holed up in a hotel room with her usual accoutrements and wrote in longhand.

On January 20, Angelou stood before 250,000 people on the steps of the Capitol building. They waved flags and cheered. Although Angelou had been performing and speaking for decades, the enormity of where she was and what she was about to do nearly overwhelmed her. Her words could help set the tone of the nation in the coming years.

"I tried not to realize where I was," Angelou said later. "I tried to suspend myself. I was afraid I might lose my composure."

President Clinton stood beside her as she began to read "On the Pulse of Morning." She spoke of hope for all of America's people—gays, the homeless, Native Americans, Eskimos, Jews, Africans, Muslims. Angelou's oratory skills, honed through years of stage work, were rousing. As she finished the last line, Clinton embraced her as the world watched on television.

The appearance catapulted Angelou into the public's consciousness like never before. Paperback sales of *Caged Bird* shot up 500 percent, hardcover book sales skyrocketed 1,500 percent, and requests for her to speak, at a reported $15,000 an appearance, overflowed. The following year, she won a Grammy award for her recorded reading of the poem. The fame had its lackluster side as well. With her books in demand again, *Caged Bird* became the third-most banned book in the nation in the 1990s. The rape scene is most often cited as the reason school libraries have pulled the book.

In 1993, Angelou published a book of essays, *Wouldn't Take Nothing for My Journey Now*, dedicated to Oprah Winfrey, whom she had met nearly a decade earlier. That year Angelou also published her first children's book, *Life Doesn't Frighten Me*, an illustrated version of one of her poems. The following year she published another children's book, *My Painted House, My Friendly Chicken and Me*, and won the Horatio Alger Award.

On the heels of such publishing success, one of Angelou's other dreams came true. She had wanted to direct since age 40 when she took a course in cinematography while in Sweden. Upon reading the script for *Down in the Delta*, she knew she had found her debut vehicle. "But of course, everything I learned 30 years ago was obsolete by the time I got a chance," Angelou said. "Halfway through reading this screenplay, I knew I wanted to do it, because it really is a simple human story—a great story. And it has within it all of the elements I've tried to deal with in my work—loss, love, fear, threat, hope, redemption."

Angelou, who was used to creating in solitude, suddenly had a cast and crew of more than 100 people around her. "It challenged me," she said. "That's an understatement. Trying to be creative in the presence of lots of people was incredible to me."

The film was an ambitious project that told the story of a black woman from Chicago whose life is a mess. She heads south with her two kids to find her roots and a new life. Released in 1997, *Down in the Delta* received mixed reviews. Angelou's directorial skills produced a competent and touching movie, although not a particularly spectacular one.

In 1995, Maya read one of her poems at the 50th anniversary of the founding of the United Nations. *A Brave and Startling Truth* described the fragility of human relations and called for peace: "We, this people, on a small and lonely planet traveling through casual space, passed a lot of stars, across a way of indifferent suns to a destination where all signs tell us it is possible and imperative that we discover a brave and startling truth," Angelou read.

For Angelou, that "brave and startling truth" was about love, born in God. Angelou's relationship with God, which began in her grandmother's home and church, had deepened over the years, and still imbues many of her poems. It invariably comes up during interviews and lectures, in which Angelou says she is still awed by God's love:

> This idea that it, this creation, creator, it, loves me, me—not me generically, but me, Maya Angelou—is almost more—it is more than I can comprehend. It fills me. It means that I am connected to every thing and every body. That's all delicious and wonderful—until I'm forced to realize that the bigot, the brute, the batterer is also a child of "it." Now, he may not know it, but I'm obliged to know that he is. I have to that is my contract.

Also in 1995, Angelou lent her poetry to the Million Man March, a Washington rally designed to encourage black men to be responsible to both their families and their communities. Angelou was one of the few women to speak at the march. She panned the crowd of men that stretched from the Capitol steps to the Washington monument and began to read words from black women to black men. They were words of their history and their hope.

The year was a busy one. A compilation of Angelou's poetry came out, called *The Complete Poems of Maya Angelou*; she played small roles in two movies—*Poetic Justice* with Janet Jackson, and *How to Make an American Quilt*; and she worked with producer Norman Lear to develop a late-night television variety/talk show that didn't make it to syndication.

Over the years, Angelou's friendship with Oprah Winfrey grew stronger. The then up-and-coming television personality first met Angelou at a function in Baltimore. Upon reading *Caged Bird*, Winfrey instantly felt she'd found a kindred spirit.

"We talked as if we had known each other our entire lives; and throughout my 20s and in the years beyond, Maya brought clarity to my life lessons," Winfrey said. "Now we have what I call a mother-sister-friend relationship."

Angelou has been a guest on *Oprah* several times, and Winfrey has thrown Angelou two huge birthday bashes. For Angelou's 65th birthday, Oprah hosted a two-day, 400-guest extravaganza at Wake Forest University. Five years later, she outdid herself with a weeklong birthday cruise for Angelou that included illustrious guests, a private party in the Florida Keys, tours of Mayan ruins, and gourmet meals.

Angelou herself is known for throwing her widely divergent friends together at parties. The odd and engaging assortment of friends she has collected over the years form a sort of second family for her.

People of all races, genders, and religions, seem to fall in love with Angelou. Her friends describe her as immeasurably loving, graceful, present, queen like. Her home is a haven for them. Food is often the way she soothes and entertains. Every Thanksgiving, she hosts a dinner for 100 of her friends cooking much of the meal herself. She collects cookbooks and competes in cooking competitions for charities, where people may pay $250 to eat her dishes. While Angelou can whip up the finest of French sauces, she often opts for good southern food like greens, fried chicken, and biscuits.

Famed for her tolerance, Angelou has little patience intolerance, and is quick to order guests to leave her house if they tell a derogatory joke. She does so with no embarrassment and no worry about disrupting her parties:

I'm convinced that the negative has power. It lives. And if you allow it to perch in your house, in your mind, in your life, it can take you over. So when the rude or cruel thing is said—the lambasting, the gay bashing, the hate—I say, "Take it all out of my house!" Those negative words climb into the woodwork and into the furniture, and the next thing you know they'll be on my skin.

Angelou is also quick to dismiss people with false modesty or people who don't value friendship as much as she does. In fact, when asked to name a personal fault, she has said, "I never make friends with anyone who does not love me back."

Angelou has a reputation as a fierce friend and an equally fierce enemy. Journalists sometimes speak of her as intimidating, proud, or critical. Interviewers are sometimes warned to address her as Dr. Angelou and to be humble. But very little has been written about Angelou that is not flattering. Most interviewers simply collect her thoughts and feelings on the movements of the day, on living with art, on her famous friends, and cite disclosures from her autobiographies. While she has received some criticism for not teaching many classes although employed as a well-paid professor at Wake Forest, for the most part, Maya Angelou's life has been analyzed only in her own words.

Joan Riley, a young black Caribbean author, says that Angelou has achieved a kind of public sainthood, that the trauma she suffered in her youth has placed her beyond criticism. Certainly, being a black woman who grew up poor and abused has made Angelou a touchy subject for thorough and honest assessment. Moreover, her very demeanor seems to elicit respect and curtails anything but glowing words from interviewers.

Angelou commands attention—when she walks into a room, heads turn. She brings with her all of the "strong, kind, and powerful" people and things she's known. She absorbs every great book, every great person, country, conversation. "I take them, and I know them, and I am them." Angelou has said. "So when I walk into a room, people know that somebody has come in—they just don't know it's 2,000 people!"

Maya and her son Guy have remained very close over the years. After Angelou left him in Ghana in 1965, Guy embarked on his own wandering life. He finished his education in Egypt and moved to Spain, where he managed a bar. Later he moved to London and ran a photo safari service. He worked on oil-drilling rigs in Kuwait and later became the first black executive at the now defunct Western Airlines.

Angelou is proud of Guy—of his independence, his success. "I'll always be a mother," she said. "That's really it. If you are really a mother you can let go . . . because love liberates. That's what it does. It says, 'I love you. Wherever you go, I love you.'"

In 1976, Guy returned to America, and he and his pregnant wife settled into Angelou's guesthouse in Sonoma, California. By the early 1980s, he had moved to Oakland, where he's been a city personnel manager for 20 years. Following his spinal cord surgery in 1982, Guy underwent several more operations. After one such surgery in the late 90s, he phoned his mother and asked if she would read him a poem while the doctors removed the stitches:

> While he was lying in the hospital, he called me one day and said, "Mom, recite *Invictus* to me." As I began, I remembered this eight-year-old to whom I had taught, "Out of the night that covers me, black as the pit from pole to pole, I thank whatever gods may be for my unconquerable soul. . . ." Through all of those years, I remember that little person, stomping around, marching like he was a soldier. And now, here he was, needing something to hold onto, something to repeat to himself.

Along the way Guy also began writing poetry, some of which was published in *Essence* magazine. He also edited an anthology of works by black writers called *My Brother's Keeper*, and in 1998, Guy Johnson's first novel was published. Angelou knew Guy loved reading and that he had dabbled in writing, but she didn't know he had books in him. "I was so surprised to find him writing novels," she said.

Standing at the Scratch Line is loosely based on the life of Guy's grandfather, Maya's father Bailey, and follows him from the turn of the century through fights with crooked politicians and mobsters. The book was well reviewed, and Guy is working on a sequel.

Guy says his mother gave him the tools:

> Due to my mother, I have had the good fortune to grow up around some of the great writers, actors, musicians and dancers of our time. The recitation of poetry and prose was an important aspect of my home life. I have benefited greatly from having a parent who valued creativity and loved reading, for she passed that love and value system along to me.

When Guy was asked how it felt to grow up in Maya Angelou's shadow, he responded, "I always thought I was standing in her light."

When she began laying bare her life to readers, Maya Angelou envisioned her autobiographies running to seven or eight books. It has been over 15 years since she last wrote an autobiography, and it appears her interest in this form of literature has waned. She has, however, been working on a book, at Oprah's suggestion, about how to live more fully, and she continues to still write poetry. She also continues to speak about life with all its triumphs and tragedies:

> Because of the routines we follow, we often forget that life is an ongoing adventure. We leave our homes for work, acting and even believing that we will reach our destinations with no unusual event startling us out of our set expectations. The truth is we know nothing. . . . Life is pure adventure, and the sooner we realize that, the quicker we will be able to treat life as art. . . .

> Life seems to love the liver of it.

RACHEL THOMAS

Exuberance as Beauty: The Prose and Poetry of Maya Angelou

INTRODUCTION

> I speak to the Black experience, but I am always
> talking about the human condition. . .
> —Maya Angelou (Braxton, 126)

Many have discussed the problematic sense of voice and audience in the works of Maya Angelou, particularly in her works of autobiography. Placing her squarely within the tradition of the slave narrative or the coming-of-age bildungsroman is, indeed, problematic. While, as a proud and well-read African-American woman, the voice of the character Maya does reflect the sass and doublespeak long associated with the prose of her people, her periodic and self-imposed detachment from social mores is more in keeping with the lonely hero of the bildungsroman than with the heroic exemplum of the people common in African-American literature (Gilbert, 85–88). Truly, Maya Angelou stands between these two traditions, and her voice never fully stems from one or the other. The wavering of her literary voice between two such opposing traditions reflects the individual distinction that is at the heart of her works. Her fractured identifications make her an exemplary voice of African-America, of the female character, and even of the Western canonical tradition in which she was educated. However, the greatest truth in her voice is that of an individual, and where her varied association with fragments of society, race, and culture make her style adherent to many traditions, her admirable story of self-discovery makes her voice unique and her appeal universal.

Displacement and Identity

> I have been devoting
> all my time to get
> Parts of you out floating
> still unglued as yet.

The lines of Angelou's poem "Here's to Adhering," characterize the process of piecing together the self-identity that spans the volumes of Maya Angelou's autobiography and poetry. When, in *Caged Bird*, Angelou describes the multiple burdens of the black female, she outlines the levels of self-acceptance through which she must pass in her own process of adhering. "The Black female. . .is caught in the tripartite crossfire of masculine prejudice, white illogical hate, and Black lack of power" (265). In this statement, she charts the course through autobiography by which she will seek and eventually develop an intact personal identity—as a woman, a black, an American, and an African, and as a member of the society of men.

Four crises of self shape Angelou's journey through the volumes of her life story: She places herself in opposition to the black community (of Stamps), the white community (of the larger world), the male gender (the men of her personal relationships), and the nation of America (the country she abandons in order to see from the outside what elements of each cultural association she will take as her own) in order to examine the societal and cultural identifiers with which she comes in contact, and to make her judgment upon them. The theme of societal displacement runs deep, and she actively embraces the opportunity for confrontation in order to distinguish not only whom her true oppressors are, but also to discern what is and is not a part of her individual persona.

The understanding of these labels comes gradually and not necessarily sequentially. Rather, they overlap as her experiences of geography and society change. For example, her time in St. Louis first opens her eyes to the possibility of strong black women in the world, but it is not until she is permanently situated in the multiracial setting of San Francisco that she can develop her persona as a proud member of the black community, having left behind the singular example of prejudicial toleration in Stamps.

Selwyn Cudjoe identifies Maya's failed marriage to Tosh Angelos as the point in her life when she faces a decision between assertion and loss of her identity. Should she allow herself to be absorbed into the larger whitened world, "effacing her own culture entirely," or should she assert her identity as part of a black culture, and as an individual (72)? Cudjoe's distinction of absorption versus identity accurately describes the tension between her associations as not only black, but also as woman, mother, female, African or American, and can be extended to apply at each transition point in her life.

Though the identification against which she positions herself changes throughout her childhood and adulthood, her pattern of choice between absorption and identification recurs. Dolly Aimee McPherson asserts that Angelou "defines herself, sometimes against, but always because of the group identity that provides her frame of reference" (29). In choosing to position herself against the prevailing group identity rather than be accepted and lose her individualism to the majority each time, she is always setting herself up to face another challenge to her identity, but also to discover the elements of her being by the remote examination of others. In this way, she perpetuates a pattern of displacement even as she is laying down a path to self-knowledge.

A geographic displacement follows that of the emotional in Angelou's autobiographies. Many have asserted the connection between her works and those of slave narrative, suggesting that Angelou's constant physical movement through the years links her to the geographic escape of her ancestors. George E. Kent understands the themes of geographic and emotional instability in African-American literature as not only factual, but purposeful, suggesting that blacks have a "relationship to all institutions devised to ward off chaos threatening human existence" (17). This implies a conscious pattern of displacement in the lives of authors such as Angelou, perhaps born from the historic need to avoid oppression on all sides. As slaves fled their masters, Angelou flees the discontents of her past, moving always toward a greater freedom of self and an eventual stable resting place.

The link is further validated in her poetry, specifically in the poem "Our Grandmothers," from Angelou's poetic work *I Shall Not Be Moved*. Here, the protagonist is trapped in a current of constant physical movement. When escaping from slavery, standing amidst an ocean and sending her children away, she is caught in a set of circumstances that she can neither control nor disregard. The scene changes with each verse, through time and space, but the woman repeats always, "I shall not be moved" (253). This paradigm of strong conviction in a sea of turmoil points to an internal stability guiding the grandmother, and also Angelou. Able to cling to an inner conviction, Angelou is displaced and, indeed, displaces herself again and again without ruin.

As a child, Angelou places herself in opposition to the black community of Stamps, Arkansas, and therefore to her own black identity. In the opening scene of *I Know Why the Caged Bird Sings*, young Marguerite faces the Colored Methodist Episcopal Church, reciting for Easter, but unable to move beyond the lines

> What you looking at me for?
> I didn't come to stay. . .

The inclusion of this scene at the opening of *Caged Bird*, straying from Angelou's typically correct chronology, states its universality in her life. Daniel Challener aptly describes the scene as an "emblematic preface that articulates the prevailing sense of displacement and homelessness apparent throughout [Angelou's autobiography]" (44). Her words outline the recurring patterns of her life on several levels: self-segregation from those that would absorb her, and a continual goal of moving on to greater goals and knowledge.

Angelou presents herself at the outset as, in some sense, actively removed from her social setting, whatever it may be. As she stands before the black congregation trying to recite the lines, her physical opposition and accompanying social displacement are counterpoint to the displacement of the whole black community in a white-biased world (Braxton, 133). Rather than settling into what seems a permanent home, young Maya rejects the slang, cuisine, and other defining features of the Stamps community. Her childish fantasies revolve around the belief that she is caught in a "black ugly dream" (*Caged Bird*, 4) from which she will awaken to a "whitened reality" (Smith, 4).

This intense opposition to her black identity stems in part from Angelou's sense of abandonment by her parents. With the arrival of a beautiful blonde, blue-eyed doll from her mother, Maya understands her skin color as wrong; she feels diminished as an African American because, in the first contact with her mother, she receives assurance of her previous conjecture that little white girls "were everybody's dream of what was right in the world" (*Caged Bird*, 4). Maya the child rejects what she sees in herself as causing her emotional pain, in Stamps and again later in her life. It is only once she discovers it is possible to wear black skin and find happiness and independence that she begins to accept it, slowly.

The blacks whom she admires in Stamps are those with a degree of independence from the white community. She admires them, though, not because of their strength as black community members, but rather because of their achievement in taking on characteristics she associates with white life: financial independence, education, and respectability. *Caged Bird's* Momma, based on Angelou's fraternal grandmother Annie, lends money to the white dentist, and is renowned in Stamps as the only black woman ever called "Mrs." by a white man (*Caged Bird*, 46). Maya admires her for the respect she garners universally. Even Momma, however, is not immune to Maya's critical inquiry—her quite tolerance of white scorn is degrading in her granddaughter's eyes. Angelou balances between respect for her grandmother's strength and disdain for her acceptance of mistreatment. This distinction exemplifies the process of external judgment which Angelou passes upon each sector of humanity she encounters: here, she rejects the Christian belief of the Stamps community that white prejudice is best borne quietly. While she eventually comes to identify with her black self on most levels, Angelou never accepts the unequal place in society she sees her Stamps role-models as allowing. Said best in her poem "Lord, in My Heart," from the work *Oh Pray My Wings Are Gonna Fit Me Well*, Angelou expresses this discontent:

> Here then is my
> Christian lack:
> If I'm struck,
> Then I'll strike back. (88)

She admires the black aristocrat Bertha Flowers for her ability to act, with the most beautiful of black skins, in a manner Angelou had thought possible only for a white person. "She acted just as refined as whitefolks in the movies and books and she was more beautiful" (*Caged Bird*, 92). Flowers's instruction in literature and tolerance opens Angelou's eyes to the realization that mastery of language and pride in self are not limited to those of light skin.

The brief stay in St. Louis prior to her meeting Bertha Flowers gives Angelou a counterpoint with which to compare the Stamps way of life. There she finds examples of strong black women standing up for themselves within the larger African-American community of St. Louis, and even in relation to the white population. These examples of brute strength, coupled with the intellectual ability and gentility of Bertha Flowers, open Angelou's eyes to the idea that she may fulfilling her dream of becoming an educated woman and a proud black American. Glimpsing the opportunity for equality in Bertha Flowers, Angelou first begins to examine her black identity as something that she will accept and in which she will eventually take pride.

Angelou does not fully accept her black identity, however, until she is placed in the wider world of San Francisco, California. When she finds herself in a predominantly white community for the first time, she also finds a new social group against which she must define herself. Here, geographic displacement heralds a new level of societal displacement in Angelou's life. Having found the possibility of being black and proud, she begins to build this part of her identity in the face of prejudice and racism in San Francisco. "In that rarefied atmosphere," she admits, "I came to love my people more" (*Caged Bird*, 209).

Angelou eventually accepts herself as black, but never her place as a black girl in the South. In fact, she does not return to the South permanently until, as an adult, she has accepted herself in her capacities as an independent, African-American woman. Only after these elements of her self-image are secure can she return to a physical place that once caged her without falling under the same set of bars. Thus, Angelou continues her geographical movement until she is emotionally whole, ending her journey in the South (in North Carolina), where she began in pieces.

The exploration of her black identity in opposition to a white world marks the second battle of absorption versus identity that Angelou faces. She latches onto the possibility of Black strength in the face of her expanding black and white world. She builds a pride in her blackness with each triumph of strength and perseverance she achieves in the white world—as the first black trolley conductor, in her managerial control of two white prostitutes, in her half-truth acceptance into the army.

The development of this identity, suggests Cudjoe, reaches a climax in her relationship to Tosh Angelos, her first husband. Having only recently discovered White culture as something beyond the realm of women's magazine advertisements, her relationship with Tosh marks the first personal interaction with a white person in which Angelou comes to see whites as equally human and as individuals. Though she has had a series of professional associations with low-down white people during her slew of short underworld careers, they lead only to her understanding of such whites as a class of "powhitetrash" similar to those living in the black community of Stamps, and therefore as separate from the gleaming white society of the advertisements. Thus, she enters her marriage with the belief that she is embarking on a path to the *Better Homes and Gardens* life that she has been taught—by white society—is the ideal of any woman. She associates the stable existence that has always eluded her in black society with white life:

> At last I was a housewife, legally a member of that enviable tribe
> of consumers whom security made fat as butter and who under
> no circumstances considered living on bread alone, because their
> husbands brought home the bacon. I had a son, a father for him,

a husband and a pretty home for us to live in. My life began to resemble a Good Housekeeping advertisement (*Singin' and Swingin'*, 31)

Her acceptance into a white consumer society does not at first seem to conflict with her African-American identity. "I was so enchanted with security and living with a person whose color or lack of it could startle me awake on an early-morning waking" (*Singin' and Swingin'*, 34). When she and Tosh do begin to conflict, she is first willing to sacrifice her outer associations with black culture in order to maintain the stability of life which she has craved since childhood. Thus, she submits to her husband's wishes that she not attend church. An internal struggle ensues between Angelou's desire for stability (which she does not associate with black culture) and her need to hold onto the black identity she has only recently accepted.

Eventually, Tosh's rejection of the religious convictions that she so closely associates with her Stamps experience leads to her to understand the importance that her religious upbringing holds for her. Her belief in whiteness—or at least marriage to whiteness—as necessary for and guaranteeing stability is broken. She takes from her failed marriage not the assertion by her people that "again a white man had taken a black woman's body and left her hopeless, helpless, and alone" (*Singin' and Swingin'*, 44), but rather the understanding that she had been wrong to surrender the bits of "territory" which had stripped her identity in both her eyes and Tosh's. She learns the centrality of her black identity as an element she must build her self-acceptance upon, and her need for the stability of its *association* in her largely rootless life. This marks the first instance of Angelou's understanding that stability and security may be found internally or abstractly, rather than geographically.

The failure of her first marriage, while sealing her acceptance of her black heritage, also marks the beginning of her active association with it. At this point in the autobiographical journey, she begins to *actively* stand for the black community with the words of childhood still on her tongue:

What you looking at me for?
I didn't come to stay. . .

She now steps into the arena of entertainment and finds a mode by which she can reach social equality—perhaps even friendship—with whites, while publicizing the beautiful culture of black America. The discovery of her talent arms her with a means of personally battling racism, and for the first time Angelou has a personal power behind her combative stance. Her intimacy with, and love for Tosh has brought Whites into the realm of individuals, rather than faceless oppressors. Her experience with Tosh allows her to appreciate not only the possibility of her friendly association with whites, but also her ability to speak for her people on equal footing with whites. She moves on to spread a message of black pride from her place on stage, and to defend black-American freedom and equality at the side of Reverend Martin Luther King Jr.

While her experience with Tosh in no way resolves the issue of Maya's confrontation with the white world, it leads her mentally to a level of security where she can move forward in building her self-confidence and understanding of her place in the world. The breakdown of her position against the white world is ever so slow and occurs in conjunction with the strengthening of Angelou's self-image as a black, a woman, and, finally, an American. Her confrontational spirit wanes only as her yearning for external identification lessens.

While motherhood is a theme that binds the volumes of Angelou's autobiography, her fundamental awareness as a woman is highlighted as the third of four crises Angelou faces in the structuring of her self-identity. This challenge is most specifically highlighted in her fourth autobiographical volume, *The Heart of a Woman*.

Noting that, in her initial explanation of the "tripartite crossfire" she has faced, she speaks from the stance of a black *woman*, one finds that the adult narrator Angelou has successfully integrated her womanhood as a positive aspect of self. However, sexuality is a source of concern for the character Maya, beginning at a young age, and the common concern about appearance is not missed in her narration. Lacking a small frame or fine features, Maya is not considered pretty as a young girl. Rather, her brother Bailey is blessed with traditionally feminine characteristics—grace, flowing curls—while Maya is simply a "too big Negro girl" (*Caged Bird*, 4), passed off jokingly by her family as the daughter of a Chinese man. This reversal is undoubtedly a source of confusion for the child, and her appearance is yet another source of displacement for Angelou.

While her opposition to womanhood is never as outright or aggressive as her confrontation of black identity and white society, she does not begin to explore, or embrace, her sexuality and the strength derived from being female until after the birth of her son, Guy.

Angelou's insecurity over her appearance is compounded at the age of eight by the rape she endures by her mother's lover. The tremendous guilt she feels, coupled with the much-too-early awakening to her sexuality, further displaces Angelou from comfort as a woman by separating her associations of sex and love entirely. Exemplifying this fact, her next sexual encounter takes place after a mere introduction to the idea of lesbianism sufficiently convinces the wholly insecure Angelou that, because of her having been moved by the vision of a friend's bare chest, she too must be a "woman lover" (*Caged Bird*, 266). She again understands her sexuality as wrong when judging by her surroundings, just as she decided her appearance to be wrong following the receipt of a white doll. As with this blonde and blue-eyed example from her childhood, Angelou finds less than sufficient reassurance or acceptance from her mother to squelch her insecurity.

The experience of Guy's birth, however, forcibly opens a door to stability that had not previously existed in Angelou's life. While Angelou does not deny her inability to fully comprehend her role as mother at the time—"just as gratefulness was confused in my mind with love, so possession became mixed up with motherhood" (*Caged Bird*, 280)—she does allude to her experiencing, for the first time, the fact that her sexuality and femaleness are innate in her identity. One particular incident relates Angelou's first encounter with her motherly instincts. Frightened that her newborn would be crushed sleeping in bed with her, Angelou begs her mother not to leave the young Guy in her bed once she falls asleep. When the practical Vivian Baxter refuses, Angelou vows to stay awake the entire night to avoid smothering the baby inadvertently. However, she awakes to the voice of her mother, and looks to find the baby sleeping safely in the crook of her arm. Instinctively, she has created a tent with her arm in which the baby sleeps:

> Mother whispered, "See, you don't have to think about doing the right thing. If you're for the right thing, then you do it without thinking" (*Caged Bird*, 281).

Vivian's assurance plants the first seed of womanly confidence in Angelou. She recognizes that, despite appearance, awkwardness, or insecurity, she is a woman without trying. The assertion by her mother that she is "for the right thing" begins to reverse the tide of self-loathing stemming from her abandonment by the same woman years earlier. If the mother who abandoned her as wrong could see her as being fundamentally right, Angelou might also understand her sexuality as fitting well.

Though she does not realize it until it is threatened, Angelou's womanhood and motherhood prove the most consistent source of inner stability throughout the external trials of her life's journey. Her need for adaptation in order to provide for her child, and the innate ability to do so which comes with being female, give her the strength of character to confront the hardship she meets. This fluidity of character helps her to survive, and the certainty of womanhood is the compass she follows in life.

If the birth of Guy is the start of Angelou's exploration into the heart of her womanhood, her acceptance of Female as a fundamental part of her identity comes with her divorce from Vusumzi Make, her second husband. In rejecting his paternalistic attitude, she again fights the battle of absorption versus identity, choosing to assert her strength as a woman rather than to have her own identity absorbed into that of her husband.

Her gradual realization of the importance that her female independence holds is characterized in the following passage from *The Heart of a Woman*:

> My position had always been that no one was responsible for my life except me. . .Of course, no man had ever tried to persuade me differently by offering the security of his protection. . .I wanted to be a wife and to create a beautiful home to make my man happy, but there was more to life than being a diligent maid and a permanent pussy (*Heart*, 167–168).

Never having had her independence challenged in adulthood, and having always been the sole protector of herself and her son, Angelou begins to note the centrality of her womanhood only when it is threatened by the complete dependence which her marriage to Make demands. Though motherhood has been one of the few constants throughout her life, she has not necessarily had the opportunity to recognize the equal significance of her identity as a strong woman and the fact that her ability to mother stems from that womanly strength. In the face of Make's attempts to control her, she discovers the third level of identity that she must secure: Maya the woman.

It is significant that Angelou's rejection of Make comes only after their arrival and settling in Africa. This continent of black skin provides an environment free from white pressure in which Angelou can explore her femaleness and eventually her American status (Hagen, 107). Ekaterini Georgoudaki explains this significance by stressing Angelou's understanding of Africa as female rather than as a place (19). She emphasizes Angelou's view of Africa as a woman showing "strength under stress" and "perseverance in a hostile world" (25). It is, therefore, likely that the acceptance begun with her real mother should be completed with Mother Africa. Angelou draws the strength to assert her independence from the earth of a strong woman beneath her feet.

She makes note, in *The Heart of a Woman*, of the generally male-dominant society still present on the continent of Africa. She comments on her first meeting with the wives of other African leaders, saying that she "didn't know then that all wives of freedom fighters lived their lives on the edge of screaming desperation" (*Heart*, 158). While one might construe this statement as a comment on the constant worry of these wives over the safety of their husbands, in Angelou's case it is more appropriate to interpret it as revealing her frustration at not being included in the freedom fight herself.

Even while preparing to assert her womanly independence, Angelou does not allow herself to fully identify with the singular label of "woman" just yet. Instead she states that

> Some black women agreed that black man had rapacious appetites, and allowed their husbands and lovers the freedom of the fields. Some other women, with knives and guns, boiling water, poison and the divorce courts proved that they did not agree with the common attitude (*Heart*, 295).

She clearly does not include herself in the "common attitude," and thus effectively presents herself as in opposition to a yet another majority. Always quick to assert the fact that she does not associate herself with the feminist movement of white American women (Gilbert, 89), Angelou then, by default, positions herself against black men alone rather than the male sex in its entirety. In her fear of absorption, she reminds the reader of her individuality as a *black* woman, and further as a woman with a distinct personality, by outlining these several modes of difference in her situation from that of the majority.

During the demanded divorce court of acquaintances in which Angelou and Make find themselves, she purposely uses profanity and "revel[s] in the rustle of discomfort" (*Heart*, 300), pushing her opposition to its fullest point. Expecting rejection, she is surprised when the court sides with her; the correctness of her strength and power as a woman is thus reinforced even in the most paternalistic of environments. The completion of her divorce marks the ultimate confirmation of her female identity.

As with her transition from the black Stamps community to the larger white-dominated community of San Francisco, Angelou's move from America to Africa gives her a new scene for confrontation, and thus provides an impetus for the quickened acceptance of one element of her identity in order to begin the battle for another. Angelou is able to accept female nature as a central part of her identity more easily because she is simultaneously faced with the question of her identity as an African versus American.

In the final volume of her autobiography, *All God's Children Need Traveling Shoes*, Angelou settles in Ghana, with the hope of ending her lifelong displacement and being accepted at last into her "home." The theme of African return is a common one in African-American literature, particularly in autobiography. In Angelou's works, this idea is present nearly from the point at which she first understands slavery as having been an institution. However, her journey to Egypt, with the cast of *Porgy and Bess* is the first instance in which Angelou recognizes her American status as a distinct identifier in her life, and one with which she must later grapple. From this point, she idealizes Africa in her mind as the geographic place where she will find herself whole again.

Africa comes to represent "home" on a number of levels for Angelou—literally, as the native land of her ancestors; symbolically, as the mother who abandoned her long ago; but also hopefully, as embodying the distant possibility for complete acceptance which she strives for continually. Maya Angelou "adopt[s] Africa as a place of peace, freedom, security, and happiness," states Ekaterini Georgoudaki (19).

Though the African backdrop gives Angelou an opportunity to explore her understanding of what it is to be African American without racial distraction, she at first positions herself mentally in opposition to the Africans amongst which she finds herself, as she has done when faced with any new cultural situation. This mental opposition again allows her to examine the culture laid out before her—and the options for identification that exist—but also puts her in a position of antagonism to the one place that has occupied her mind as an ending point for her journey of displacement. In *The Heart of a Woman*, Angelou describes herself in relation to the story of Brer Rabbit, a long-enduring symbol of African-American survival. When her coworkers at a Cairo newspaper suggest she move her desk to an empty library supposedly for the sake of learning Arabic, Angelou relates the story of Brer Rabbit and the Briar Patch, identifying herself as Brer Rabbit and characterizing the Egyptians as the man who threatens Brer Rabbit with the "worst thing" (*Heart*, 277). In this case, it is the library's volumes of English text—a familiar sight from her American upbringing—that represent the niche (the "worst thing") in which Angelou is most comfortable. As her world of books sheltered Angelou from white racism and oppression as a child in Stamps and a young adult in San Francisco, it also buffers her from prejudicial treatment of another sort in Africa. This African versus American usage of the tale is ironic, given that the man opposing Brer Rabbit generally represents the white oppression of African Americans. Here, Angelou pinpoints the Africans of her promised land as nearly synonymous with the oppression she knew in America, though for different reasons. She recognizes that the geographic place she had dreamed of is not without imperfections as a possible home.

Despite these instances of conflict in Egypt, Angelou reverses her lifelong pattern of wary examination upon reaching Ghana. For the first time, she throws herself into the society and culture of Africa—trying, it would seem, to *make* Africa embrace her. The Ghanian society, however, reacts to her with the same indifference of the Stamps community years earlier: "It closed in around us, as a real mother embraces a stranger's child. Warmly, but not too familiarly" (*Caged Bird*, 7). She is embraced by a slew of colorful characters, but always as a visiting American of individual interest, and never as an African. Angelou and her fellow expatriates actively reject their American identities by moving to Africa and embracing Ghana's leader as their own, but find that they are unable to completely dislodge their association. Eventually—and ironically—each finds the greatest solace in the company of fellow Americans. Again, Angelou accepts her American identity where she finds it a rarity, just as she had done as a black girl in white San Francisco.

Just as she moved toward accepting her black identity in childhood by finding individual black examples of the independence she so desired, Angelou likewise is eased in the acceptance of her American identity by the African-American examples she encounters and examines in Africa. In this case, however, it is the reminders of an abandoned Black America that tug at her heartstrings and lead her to recognize the importance of the "American" in her label as an African American. David DuBois, her companion in Egypt, and Julian Mayfield, fellow expatriate in Ghana, offer support to Angelou in the face of mounting difficulty in foreign surroundings. The aid from and reminiscence evoked by these Americans—even as African Americans—helps her realize that abandoning America for Africa does not accomplish her goal of self-knowledge. Rather, she must reconcile the two identifiers within her makeup, as they are perhaps those that most define her place within the society of men.

Angelou's divorce from Make in some way foreshadows her experience in Ghana while searching for an elusive home. Upon her accepting his offer of marriage, Make declared, "This is the joining of Africa and Africa-America!" (*Heart*, 141). She marries without any personal knowledge of the African man, accepting the idea of a life with him—"a life beckoning adventure and Africa" (*Heart*, 140). The eventual failure of this bond suggests the inability for African America, separated so long ago, to ever fully reunite with the homeland of Africa. Angelou, as a character within her life, fails to recognize this significance at the time, but as author, she prepares her reader for the disappointment she expresses later.

Her final realization that Africa will not provide a serum for her lifelong restlessness comes at an unexpected point, after she has met with the extended family of her servant boy, Kojo:

> I drank and admitted to a boundless envy of those who remained
> on the continent, out of fortune or perfidy. Their countries had

been exploited and their cultures had been discredited by colonialism. Nonetheless, they could reflect through their priests and chiefs on centuries of continuity. . . .I doubted if I, or any Black from the diaspora, could really return to Africa (*Traveling Shoes*, 76).

Perhaps it is her sheer confusion over the encounter that makes her recognize her inability to truly flesh with the African culture around her. More likely though, it is the display of familial and cultural continuity that seems so foreign to her patterns of self-inflicted and culturally imposed displacement.

Selwyn Cudjoe suggests that Angelou does, in fact, leave Ghana more African than when she had arrived, saying that her "identification is complete and the link is made" (Lindberg-Seyersted, 76). While her admission of failure in trying to find a perfect Africa might appear to imply her complete failure at assimilation, one must not overlook the fact that African identification is indeed still a significant part of Angelou's heritage. Her experience in the small village of Keta offers validation of her African identity in some sense. Angelou is recognized as a descendant of Africa and relation of the tribal women, but also lamented as one irrevocably lost from their society. The incident clarifies the boundaries of Angelou's African and American identities, and leads her to accept both as the final pieces of self in need of adherence. Reflecting on this experience while preparing to return into America, Angelou remarks:

Many years earlier I, or rather someone very like me and certainly related to me, had been taken from Africa by force. This second leave-taking would not be so onerous, for now I knew my people had never completely left Africa. We had sung it in our blues, shouted it in our gospel, and danced the continent in our breakdowns (*Traveling Shoes*, 208).

She ends her search for personal identity with the knowledge that the nature of her parts makes a single geographic home impossible—her Black skin keeps her from full comfort in a white-controlled America; her femaleness makes her unsuited for a male-dominated Africa; and her American character makes her unable to completely assimilate in Africa despite the attempt. However, though the sum of her parts makes such a *physical* place of belonging impossible, they also render one unimportant. The bonds of identification, which hold her being intact, also tie her tightly to the whole of humanity. Thus, Angelou can return to America, and eventually to the South, without feeling the oppression of displacement that plagued her youth. The peace she finds in self-knowledge leads her to identify as human above all other things.

MOTHERHOOD AS STABILITY

Angelou's autobiography describes a series of forced and voluntary geographic disruptions that separate her experiences. One may posit that, through her confrontational stance toward life, *she* perpetuates her displacement with greater success than any society in which she finds herself. How, then, is it possible that Maya Angelou should emerge as one of the strongest and most successful characters to grace contemporary literature? Her ability to continually slough off external modes of stability implies an unshaken internal sense of stability that guides her through tribulation, like that of the grandmother in her poem, serving as a compass through hardship.

The experience of motherhood is that source of internal constancy which Angelou looks to for support and purpose while floundering between her various modes of identity. The constancy of her motherhood and the continual companionship of her son give Angelou not only a sense of permanency as she dismantles and restructures her self, but also a sense of purpose when her mind otherwise seeks only to flee its surroundings. It is simultaneously a steadying element, allowing her to disregard external stabilizers in her search for identity, and also one that causes her to continually seek complete stability in the future, for the sake of her son.

She gives birth to her only child at the same period in life when she begins to actively seek identification. Symbolically, she gives birth to her changeling self at the time of Guy's birth. Thus, as Guy grows through his mother's volumes, Angelou also matures, increasing her self-awareness in a manner not dissimilar from that of her young son. The period of self-discovery chronicled in Angelou's autobiography begins, in earnest, when she is 17 years of age and ends with the independence of her newly matured son when he reaches the age of 17. The parallel between mother and child provides a sense of continuity across the pages, but also gives Angelou an opportunity to view *herself* in the kind of remote sense that she uses to examine her surroundings. The example and experience of her son are the ultimate window to self-comprehension available to Angelou, and it is therefore highly significant that the two egos remain intertwined throughout her phases of self-acceptance.

As with any individual whose childhood lacked the security of parental involvement, Angelou finds parenthood difficult at times, and often sees her own insecurity in her son. She attempts to be all things to Guy—mother, father, sister, brother—in order to allay the possibility of his feeling alone as she did. At the same time, reconciliation with the mother who abandoned her is made possible because she comes to understand Vivian's past actions when she finds herself in similar circumstances. When, in *Gather Together in My Name*, her son is abducted by a baby-sitter, Angelou unwittingly faces a situation in which Guy understands himself as having been abandoned, not unlike her own abandonment at the age of three (192):

> I stood holding him while he raged at being abandoned. . . Separate from my own boundaries, I had not known before that he had and would have a life beyond being my son, my pretty baby, my cute doll, my charge. . .I began to understand that uniqueness of the person. He was three and I was nineteen, and never again would I think of him as a beautiful appendage of myself (*Gather*, 192).

Guy reacts to abandonment in a way in which Angelou was never allowed to do—with forceful emotion. This and several other incidents in Guy's life allow Angelou to experience again the emotions of her childhood, examining them from a more mature stance and subsequently coming to terms with them. The realization of her own motherly misunderstanding leads Angelou to recognize how her own mother could have misunderstood the responsibility of motherhood when abandoning her two children.

While motherhood is a continuous thread in Angelou's autobiography, the embodiment of the theme varies. The closeness of Angelou's relationship with Guy lessens as they each mature. Her need to associate with her child is reduced as she comes to term with the issues of insecurity she has held onto from her own childhood, and the immediate association with his experiences decreases as she finds and accepts her own identity. Further, the strength of her relationship with Vivian increases with Angelou's own comprehension of her role as mother.

The final split in identity between mother and son comes once Guy has left Angelou's home in Ghana and moved on to the University. In a decisive scene—one of the few repeated in two volumes—Guy declares his love for his mother, but also his independence (*Traveling Shoes*, 185). As he departs, Guy comments to Angelou, "Maybe now you'll have a chance to grow up" (*Heart*, 324). His insight is significant, alluding to the nearly formed identity his mother has cultivated in his presence but not yet tested on her own. Angelou's response, though reflecting her immediate surprise and confusion, also clarifies the separation: "How can he love me? He doesn't know me, and

I sure as hell don't know him" (*Traveling Shoes*, 186). Though she has known and understood her life through his to this point, Angelou has now constructed a separate and intact identity, and thus no longer needs to, or can know her son's identity, in the same way that one can never know another's experience fully. While her role as mother does not end per se, its importance as a source of stability is gone, and Maya Angelou steps forth as an individual.

THE LANGUAGE OF SELF-IDENTITY

> To read Angelou is to hear and see and smell
> and state and feel a world.
> —Daniel Challener (45)

The language with which Maya Angelou spins her web of prose and poetry affords a palette of immense color and sensation to shade the images of her experience. Her talent with metaphor and simile leads the reader to find the most satisfying insights into her life in the most abstract of descriptions.

She faithfully includes the *sensation* of her life rather than simply spelling out her emotional state at any one moment, and one appreciates her detail all the more for the private thoughts stealthily imparted. In *Traveling Shoes*, she illustrates her infatuation with the Ghanaian people—indeed, her anticipation of having come home—by explaining her abstract impression of them:

> I was captured by the Ghanaian people. Their skins were the colors of my childhood cravings: peanut butter, licorice, chocolate and caramel (20).

Here, she does not express her belief in Africa as home in an outright manner, yet the mention of her childhood "cravings" is understood as implying not only young Marguerite's sweet tooth, but also adult Maya's tender cravings for belonging.

One cannot help but note her linguistic style when reading Angelou's collective works. The choice of words is clearly one of great import for the author, not only for the sake of conveying the correct impression, but also because of her fundamental belief in the importance of language. At a young age, an inherent love of books and the influence of Bertha Flowers brought her to the understanding that "language is a man's way of communicating with his fellow man and it is language alone which separates him from the lower animals" (*Caged Bird*, 95). The importance she places on the power of accurate expression motivates Angelou's careful word choice and shapes her unique and beautiful style.

The importance of language not only is the force behind Angelou's works, it is also a fundamental message within them. As that which allows one to communicate with others, language is a defining element of the individual. In relating her journey toward self-identity, Maya Angelou expresses the importance of words in identifying oneself. Particularly in the attention to naming found in her autobiographies, one recognizes her message that language is a mode of self-definition.

Across the five volumes of her life, her name changes numerous times. She begins with the given name of Marguerite Johnson, and as her personality and company change, she moves through the monikers My, Maya, Rita, Ritie, and Maya Angelos, eventually settling on Maya Angelou. The singular importance of her name becomes clear in *Caged Bird*, when she resorts to violence after being misnamed by an employer, Mrs. Cullinan. Dolly Aimee McPherson clarifies the importance of the name to Angelou as a "symbol of her tentative uniqueness; where Maya is wholly unsure of her identity, the very wording of her name sometimes stands as the only certainty she has regarding herself" (30). Being misnamed by another implies that she is not understood or recognized as an individual, and Angelou does not stand for being renamed without her permission. Thus, she alone controls her developing individualism. She gives this same respect and freedom to her son in allowing him to choose his own name. Though she gives him the name Clyde as an infant, he prefers Guy, and Angelou respects this preference religiously. For Angelou, her name is—even in its changing form—a defining element of which she is sure, and a base upon which she might build her personal identity.

Angelou is also careful to respect the linguistic diversity of the characters in her autobiography, giving credence to the idea that she sees language as defining individuals. She painstakingly preserves her mother's jive talk and the scatology of her "errring" father. Her attention to spoken conversation also reflects the insight that written language is not enough to express oneself fully. "For Angelou," says McPherson, "the mission of autobiography is bound up with the magic of the spoken word and the oral tradition" (156). Again, the early lessons of Bertha Flowers ring out through Angelou's works: "Words mean more than what is set down on paper. It takes human voice to infuse them with the shades of deeper meaning" (*Caged Bird*, 95). Indeed, the experience of Angelou's poetry magnifies her affinity for oral rhythm and the very sound of words. Where her poetry has been criticized for a lack of structured thought, one cannot fault the pure rhythm and delectable sound of its performance. The combination of written line and spoken word reaches the pinnacle of individual expression to which Angelou aspires in her daily life.

For Angelou, the significance of language is not only as self-defining, but also the external conveyance of that self-definition. It is not enough to name oneself and one's personality; one must also impart that self-image correctly to the outside world in order for it to be recognized and accepted as real. Angelou's interest in dictionaries displays her great preoccupation with being *correctly* understood. During the international journeys of *Singin' and Swingin' and gettin' Merry Like Christmas*, she obtains a dictionary at every stop, learning enough of the local language to express herself as needed. She sees language as the link between humans, and wants always to link herself to those around her. Her early love of Shakespeare, who was scandalous in his crossing of color lines, reflects Angelou's belief in the power of words to transcend human differences. In her childish manner, she forgives herself the love of a white man by concluding, "After all, he had been dead so long it couldn't matter to anyone any more" what race he had been (*Caged Bird*, 14). Translated through the eyes of the adult Angelou, the sentiment implies a hope, a belief that her messages of individual importance and self-acceptance will be carried color-blind through the language of her autobiography and poetry.

EXUBERANCE AS BEAUTY: THE POETRY OF MAYA ANGELOU

The poetry of the "phenomenal woman," Maya Angelou, distills the emotions and experiences of her lifetime, with which she filled five autobiographical volumes, to a remarkably small compilation of verses. She uses the poetic form for the purpose of case and character study, pulling themes and insights from her autobiographies for the sake of further examination and explanation. Where her autobiographies describe in detail the events of her existence, her poetry captures the essence, the raw impressions of her memory. Though her colloquial form and lack of traditional style have been criticized, one must credit her success in compiling a poetry of sensation.

Angelou has developed a habit of alternating the publication of autobiographical and poetic volumes. One may therefore view her collections of poetry as partial companions to the autobiographies that precede them. Her poetry is a mode through which she can cultivate the personal reality she has formed from the experience of autobiographical events (Ramsey, 81). For example, a scene from *Gather Together in My Name* finds Angelou amidst a group of dope addicts, being shown by a junkie friend the horrifying effects of the drug. Her prose description provides a clear message: "One man's generosity [in revealing the horrors of drug addiction] pushed me safely away from the edge" (*Gather*, 213). She even seems to prompt herself into poetic examination with the line "The senses of sound, taste, and touch had disappeared, but I had never seen so clearly or smelled so acutely" (*Gather*, 212). Subsequently, her later collection of poetry, *And Still I Rise*, also includes a poem on the subject. "Junkie Monkey Reel" concentrates on those formerly lost sights and sounds in the physical disintegration of a junkie:

> Shoulders sag,
> The pull of weighted needling.
> Arms drag, smacking wet in soft bone
> Sockets.
>
> Knees thaw,
> Their familiar magic lost. Old bend and
> Lock and bend forgot.
>
> Teeth rock in fetid gums.
> Eyes dart, die, then float in
> Simian juice.
>
> Brains reel,
> Master charts of old ideas erased. The
> Routes are gone beneath the tracks
> Of desert caravans, pre-slavery
> Years ago.
>
> Dreams fail,
> Unguarded fears on homeward streets
> Embrace. Throttling in a dark revenge
> Murder is its sweet romance.
>
> How long will
> This monkey dance?

The spotty description of physical collapse and the broken rhythm of the lines reflect the wrecked human they describe. Her mixture of physical description with sound-evoking phrases aims at conjuring a correct awareness above a logical comprehension. In this manner, Angelou hones in on the impressions left in her memory after the factual reality of a scene has been described in autobiographical terms, creating a thumbnail sketch of her emotional understanding at a given time.

Her explorations are not, however, reserved only for the most gut wrenching of experiences. Lyman Hagen posits that Angelou's poems are "written for people, not other poets" (121), and her work is therefore reflective of common experience—as seen from an atypical perspective. Thus, her style may be better appreciated when read with an unfocused lens rather than one attuned to structural correctness. She writes most often of the everyday, bringing out the color and rhythm that one might otherwise overlook, or of the emotional threads common in her life, and captures the sensible aspects of those fleeting sentiments. Angelou also plays with one's familiar associations, mixing common with radical for the sake of creating the most accurate sensation.

The title of her first poetic volume, *Just Give Me a Cool Drink of Water 'Fore I Diiie*, comes from a poem that beautifully utilizes the everyday in forming a complex sensation. This phrase, from a poem simply entitled "No No No No," speaks quite literally of a mundane action, and the simple description of cool water evokes an image in the mind's eye and a sensation in one's imagination. Angelou's experiences, however, are never so simple, and one could argue that no person's are. Continuing past the simple sensation, she juxtaposes the commonplace and the shock of death, leading the audience to a heightened sensational understanding. The single phrase, as well as the entire poem, is explained by Angelou as referring to her belief that "we as individuals. . .are still so innocent that we think if we asked our murderer just before he puts the final wrench upon the throat, 'Would you please give me a cool drink of water?' he would do so. That's innocence. It's lovely" (Hagen, 124). The image is then one of innocence fading away with the lengthening "diiie." Complex and colorful sensations such as this are at the root of Angelou's poetry, and her ability to express the nuances of human experience in vibrant color is perhaps the most remarkable aspect of it.

Works Cited

Angelou, Maya. *I Know Why the Caged Bird Sings*. New York: Random House, 1969.

———. *Gather Together in my Name*. New York: Random House, 1974.

———. *Oh Pray My Wings Are Gonna Fit Me Well*. New York: Random House, 1975.

———. *Singin' and Swingin' and Gettin' Merry Like Christmas*. New York: Random House, 1976.

———. *The Heart of a Woman*. New York: Bantam Books, 1981.

———. *All God's Children Need Traveling Shoes*. New York: Random House, 1986.

———. *I Shall Not Be Moved*. New York: Random House, 1990.

Braxton, Joanne M. "A Song of Transcendence: Maya Angelou." Black Women Writing Autobiography: A Tradition Within a Tradition. Philadelphia: Temple University, 1989.

Challener, Daniel D. "When a Whole Village Raises a Child: *I Know Why the Caged Bird Sings*." *Stories of Resilience in Childhood: The Narratives of Maya Angelou, Maxine Hong Kingston, Richard Rodriguez, John Edgar Wideman, and Tobias Wolff*. New York: Garland Publishing, Inc., 1997.

Cudjoe, Selwyn R. "Maya Angelou and the Autobiographical Statement." *Black Women Writers (1950-1980): A Critical Evaluation*, edited by Mari Evans. New York: Bantam, 1984.

Georgoudaki, Ekaterini. *Race, Gender, and Class Perspectives in the Works of Maya Angelou, Gwendolyn Brooks, Rita Dove, Nikki Giovanni, and Audre Lorde*. Thessaloniki: Aristotle University of Thessaloniki, 1991.

Gilbert, Susan. "Maya Angelou's *I Know Why the Caged Bird Sings*: Paths to Escape." *Mount Olive Review* 1:1 (Spring 1987): 39–50.

Hagen, Lyman B. *Heart of a Woman, Mind of a Writer, and Soul of a Poet*. New York: University Press of America, Inc, 1997.

Kent, George E. "Maya Angelou's I Know Why the Caged Bird Sings and the Black Autobiographical Tradition," *African American Autobiography: A Collection of Critical Essays*. Prentice Hall, 1993.

Lindberg-Seyersted, Brita. "Maya Angelou and the Homeland: One African-American Woman's Encounter with Africa." *Black and Female: Essays on*

Writing by Black Women in the Diaspora. Oslo: Scandinavian University Press, 1994.

McPherson, Dolly Aimee. "Autobiography As the Evocation of the Spirit." In *Order out of Chaos: The Autobiographical Works of Maya Angelou.* New York: Peter Lang, 1989.

————. "The Significance of Maya Angelou." In *Order out of Chaos: The Autobiographical Works of Maya Angelou.* New York: Peter Lang, 1989.

Ramsey, Priscilla R. "Transcendence: The Poetry of Maya Angelou." *A Current Bibliography on African Affairs* 17:2 (1984–85): 139–153.

Smith, Sidonie Ann. "The Song of the Caged Bird: Maya Angelou's Quest for Self-Acceptance." *Southern Humanities Review* 7:4 (Fall 1973).

SUSAN GILBERT

Maya Angelou's I Know Why the Caged Bird Sings: *Paths to Escape*

Maya Angelou's first autobiographical book, *I Know Why the Caged Bird Sings* (1970), opens in church on Easter Sunday with the child dressed up in a lavender taffeta dress lovingly tucked by "Momma," her grandmother. She hopes to wake from her "black ugly dream" (p. 4) to "look like one of the sweet little white girls who were everybody's dream of what was right with the world" (p. 4). The book closes with the heroine a sixteen-year-old mother, unmarried, who has gazed on her beautiful baby afraid to handle him until one night her mother puts the baby in bed beside her. Though she fears she will roll over and crush him, Maya wakes to find him sleeping safely by her side under the tent of covers she has made with her arm. Her mother whispers comfortingly, "See, you don't have to think about doing the right thing, if you're for the right thing, then you do it without thinking" (p. 281).

The writer neither wishes to be white nor fears for her black son. From the conflicts of black and white worlds and from the conflicts of styles at her rural religious Grandmother, "Momma," and her streetwise urban mother, she has found the strengths that will lead her beyond them both. But she has not done it "without thinking." Between the years when she was the sixteen-year-old mother, in 1944, and when as a woman of forty-two, in 1970, she published her book, she did a great deal of thinking about "doing the right thing" and did her thinking through a very varied career and wide experience of the world. The reader of the book must deal throughout with the dual

From *Moubt Olive Review* 1:1. © 1987 by Mount Olive College. Reprinted by permission.

perspective of the child, growing to consciousness of herself and the limits of her world, and the author, experienced, confident, and didactic.

It is a story of hurt, and loneliness, and anger, and love. The first memory is of separation; when she was three and her brother Bailey four, they were sent alone by train from California, where their parents had broken up their marriage, to Stamps, Arkansas, to live with their paternal grandmother. Fixed forever in the woman's consciousness are her love for her beautiful, clever brother, their grief, and their dreams of the mother who has sent them away. Intertwined with these memories is the enormous presence of the grandmother, "Momma," a shopkeeper, a devcut Christian who prays morning and evening. By her faith she endures this world, for whose injustice she has no explanation to give the children, and hopes for her reward and retribution in the next world. The child sees and the author remembers the crushing poverty of those farm workers who trudge through Momma's store, hopeful and singing in the morning, bone weary and no richer at evening.

The whites of Stamps live across town and appear in the earliest memories only in scattered terrible vignettes: of nights when the Klan rides and all the black men hide, some in the chicken droppings under their homes, her Uncle Willie in the bottom of a barrel of potatoes; of days when "po-white-trash" girls call the dignified grandmother "Annie" and mock her in word and obscene gesture; of a grammar school graduation day robbed of its luster by the careless hurt of a white speaker, a politician, who promises new laboratories for the white high school and a paved sports field for the black.

At eight she goes with her brother to live with their mother in St. Louis. Here she is introduced to the ways of street-wise urban blacks with laws independent of the white dominant culture. It is a worldly rich environment. Their gay and beautiful mother charms her children with her singing and dancing as she charms the patrons of the bars. And she turns the other cheek to no one. Her gang of fierce brothers hold a covenant of loyalty as strong as that of the church brethren of Arkansas, but utterly different in its rules of reciprocity. The children at this stage belong to neither world but live in awe of their mother, never secure that she will be really there forever. And Maya, at age eight, is first fondled then raped by her mother's boyfriend. In the court of white justice he is found guilty, given a year's sentence, allowed to go free the same night of the trial. In the other court of the black streets the retribution is more terrible. He is kicked to death.

Maya and Bailey return to Stamps. She suffers guilt for having caused the man's death and the separation of her brother from the mother he adores. For a year she retreats to silence, one of the most terrible of the "Silences" that women writers have described.

That she emerged from this silence, Angelou attributes to the strength of Momma, who finds her a sympathetic adult friend and who later, bravely takes the children to California to their mother's guardianship, and, far beyond Momma, to her mother, Vivian Baxter, a force not daunted by sexual or racial prejudice: "To describe my mother would be to write about a hurricane in its perfect power" (p. 58). It is strength imparted with little tenderness; it is strength to endure hurts, not a strength which can protect her from them. The strengths and weaknesses of the family and the relationship of the girl to her family are the most important topics of discussion about the book, to which we will return.

The last year the book recounts is tumultuous. Maya spends a summer with her father and his new girl friend and feels close to neither. On a day trip to Mexico with her father she sees him relax in a Mexican bar, a great man, tall, handsome, funny, admired by an easy crowd, and imagines the man he might have been in another culture. She drives him back dead drunk, she who had never driven a car, in a feat of success born of desperation and courage. Then after a fight with the father's girl friend, she is dumped at someone else's house, and wanders off to sleep in a junk yard of abandoned cars and to awake to find herself in a community of homeless, run-away children. It is an odd setting for Eden but an idyll of the Golden Age nonetheless. Under the benign rule of a tall boy, "Bootsie," there was "no stealing"; "everyone worked at something," collecting bottles, mowing lawns, odd jobs. "All money was held by Bootsie and used communally" (p. 246).

The experience has a crucial place in the work. Angelou writes:

> After a month my thinking processes had so changed that I was hardly recognizable to myself. The unquestioning acceptance by my peers had dislodged the familiar insecurity. Odd that the homeless children, the silt of war frenzy, could initiate me into the brotherhood of man. After hunting down unbroken bottles and selling them with a white girl from Missouri, a Mexican girl from Los Angeles and a Black girl from Oklahoma, I was never again to sense myself so solidly outside the pale of the human race. The lack of criticism evidenced by our ad hoc community influenced me, and set a tone of tolerance for my life (p. 247).

The brotherhood of man is a distant fellowship. With the sense of tolerance comes no closeness or love. When she returns to her mother's house, the good-by's are simple and the welcome casual. Her oldest intimacy, with her brother Bailey, in ruptured first by his growing identification with "a group of slick street boys" (p. 249) then by his leaving the house to live with a white prostitute.

Maya lives in lonely uncertainty over approaching womanhood and dismay over her looks. However universal the experience, it does not make any young person feel close to others. In a desperate attempt to affirm her sexuality, she accosts a neighbor boy. After one sexual encounter—without feeling, without a word being spoken—she is pregnant. It is a last mark of the isolation in which she has lived that no one notices her pregnancy until she tells her parents of it, in her eight month.

If they have not protected her, they do not desert her, but give her care and encouragement. Maya Angelou will be a loving mother without having known tender love as a child. The book is dedicated to: "My son, Guy Johnson and all the strong black birds of promise who defy the odds and gods and sing their songs."

It is our task now to see where this book fits into several literary traditions, especially a tradition of Southern literature. For background and locale, it's hard to be more Southern than Stamps, Arkansas; St. Louis is debatable; California is OUT. Although Maya Angelou has returned to the South to become Reynolds Professor at Wake Forest, it is by a very circuitous route.

Her career, since the close of *I Know Why the Caged Bird Sings*, has made her a citizen of the world. Her works have been among all strata of humanity. The last of her teenage years she spent on the streets of California, where she was waitress, barmaid, dishwasher, nightclub entertainer, prostitute, and madam, and where she barely escaped a life of drug addiction. From this life she became a part of a world tour of *Porgy and Bess*. She has since been actress, dancer, and producer of shows for Broadway and TV. She has been journalist and editor, poet and author of her autobiographical books. She has lived and worked in Africa. She has served as a coordinator for the Southern Christian Leadership Conference. She has been university administrator and professor in Ghana, in California, in Kansas, and at Wake Forest. She holds honorary degrees from a dozen institutions.

The South that she lived in, Stamps, Arkansas, and that her kinsmen close and distant fled, makes part of her past. But she has been eager to put as much distance between herself and its white bourgeoisie traditions in literature as in life. The only black she speaks of with real scorn in this book is the father's priggish girl friend who apes the ways of middle class white women. She is a "small tight woman from the South" who "kept the house clean with the orderliness of a coffin;" who "was on close terms with her washing machine and ironing board;" who "had all the poses of the Black bourgeoisie without the material bases to support the postures" (p. 221). With more pity but no closer identification, she recounts that the poor black girls of Stamps were marked by the trivial traditions of Southern white women: "Ridiculous and even ludicrous. But Negro girls in small Southern towns, whether poverty-stricken or just munching along on a few of life's necessities, were given as extensive and irrelevant preparations for adulthood as rich white girls shown in magazines," the irrelevancies of "mid-Victorian values" (p. 101). With money earned picking cotton and with fingers too coarse for the work, they yet bought tatting or embroidery thread, and Maya herself has "a lifetime's supply of dainty doilies that would never be used in sacheted dresser drawers" (p. 101).

Although in ceasing to be Marguerite Johnson of Stamps, Arkansas, and in becoming Maya Angelou the writer, she denies the traditions—for blacks or for women—of the white South, the same themes most often called Southern fill her work. None, of course, is exclusively or originally Southern, and looking at the other traditions her work pertains to makes this very clear.

Speaking of her years in Africa and her marriage to an African, Angelou said that Ghana taught her to see the survival of distinctly African ways among the Afro-Americans. These affect her portrayal of character, individually and collectively. In *I Know Why the Caged Bird Sings* she describes Momma's reluctance to be questioned or to tell all she knows as her "African-bush secretiveness and suspiciousness" which has been only "compounded by davery and confirmed by centuries of promises made and promises broken" (p. 189). She relates the habits of address, calling neighbors "Uncle," "Sister," "Cousin" to a heritage of tribal belonging.

As a writer she says she works from her ear, from listening to her people's cadences and habits of speech. Here she is like other Southern writers, Faulkner, Welty, O'Connor, Lee Smith whose works capture the language as spoken in particular places by particular people; she differs from them in her insistence on the uniqueness of black American speech. Here and throughout her work Angelou regards language as the means of black survival and of triumph: "It may be enough, however, to have it said that we survive in exact relationship to the dedication of our poets (include preachers, musicians and blues singers)" (p. 180). But she nowhere limits herself to the tongues of black Arkansas or ghetto streets. One critic has praised her "avoidance of a monolithic Black language" and the fact that she "does not overburden black communicants with clumsy versions of homespun black speech" (p. 35). In the white high school she attended in San Francisco, Angelou became conscious that she would use two languages: "We learned to slide out of one language and into another without being conscious of the effort. At school, in a given situation, we might respond with That's not unusual." But in the street, meeting the same situation, we easily said, 'It be's like that sometimes'" (p. 219). I have said that the point of view of the book goes back and forth between that of the inexperienced girl and the experienced writer. The language also moves between a strong, colloquial simplicity and a sometimes over-blown literary mannerism. Though she does not over-use black folk speech, she never errs when she uses it as she does in such literary passages as this one, describing her self-pride on graduation day: "Youth and social approval allied themselves with me and we trammeled memories of slights and insults. The wind of our swift passage remodeled my features. Lost tears were pounded to mud and then to dust. Years of withdrawal were brushed aside and left behind, as hanging ropes of parasitic moss" (p. 167). (Whether this is more embarrassing to Southern literature than the false inflections of Southern accents offered us by Hollywood or TV—it's for you to judge!).

The literary traditions not often allied to Southern literature which undergird this work are those of a long Western tradition of the *Bildungeroman*—a novel, often autobiographical, of a young person's growing up and finding his way among the traditions and values of the family and culture in which he or she is reared—and a long tradition in this country of Afro-American autobiography. In a sense both come together in this book; some critics have referred to it inter-changeably as "novel" and autobiography. But the traditions are diametrically opposite in the ways the hero or heroine is portrayed.

In the *Bildungeroman* the loneliness of the hero is expected. Youth is self-conscious; the hero feels that the values of his family and culture are oppressive to him; he must make his escape. It is an international genre including Goethe's *Wilhelm Meister* and James Joyce's *A Portrait of the Artist as a Young Man*, with outstanding examples in Southern literature, Thomas Wolfe's *Look Homeward, Angel* and Richard Wright's *Native Son*. It influences women's works like Kate Chopin's *The Awakening*, and with the publication of this first of Angelou's works in 1970 and a host of other important books that appeared in the same decade, it affects a vital new tradition in black women's writings.

Before the publication in 1940 of Wright's *Native Son*, fiction by American black writers constituted a smaller and less important body of work than the long tradition of Afro-American autobiographies arising from the narratives of escaped or redeemed slaves. In these autobiographies, the primary mode of black American prose, the role of the hero is altogether different, not a lonely misfit, not a rejector of this people but their exemplum. One critic, Selwyn R. Cudjoe, says that the authority of these writings derives from the impersonality of the hero-narrator:

> . . . the Afro-American autobiographical statement as a form
> tends to be bereft of any excessive subjectivism and mindless

egotism. Instead, it presents the Afro-American as reflecting a much more *im-personal* condition, the autobiographical subject emerging as an almost random member of the group, selected to tell his/her tale. As a consequence, the Afro-American autobiographical statement emerges as a public rather than a private gesture, *me-ism* gives way to *our-ism* and superficial concerns about *individual subject* usually give way to the collective subjection of the group. The autobiography, therefore, is objective and realistic in its approach and is presumed generally to be of service to the group.

This critic, Cudjoe, lumps together autobiography and fiction: "Autobiography and fiction, then, are simply different means of arriving at or (re)cognizing the same truth: the reality of American life and the position of the Afro-American subject in that life. Neither genre should be given a privileged position in our literary history and each should be judged on its ability to speak honestly and perceptively about Black experience in this land" (p. 8).

Asked this question, "Do you consider your quartet to be autobiographical novels or autobiographies?" Angelou replied, "They are autobiographies," and she went on to define her intent there as reporting on a collective, not a lone individual's story. "When I wrote *I Know Why the Caged Bird Sings*, I wasn't thinking so much about my own life or identity. I was thinking about a particular time in which I lived and the influences of that time on a number of people. I kept thinking, what about that time? What were the people around young Maya doing? I used the central figure—myself—as a focus to show how one person can make it through those times."

Whether we call the work "fiction or "autobiography" *does* really matter more than just giving English teachers something to argue about. Different traditions affect the stance of the writer to her work and the responses of the reader. Especially on the most important questions of debate about this work, the nature of the family or group she portrays and the nature of the relationship of the central character to that group, the two traditions we have looked at pose different solutions. In a *Bildungeroman*—or apprenticeship novel—we expect detachment from or rejection of the group mores. In the tradition of black autobiography here described we expect total or unconscious absorption in the group. The role of the black woman in this tradition has been called that of "an all-pervading absence" (Cudjoe, p. 7). Few of many thousand such autobiographies written were by or about women. In those written by men they play a distinctly subservient role: "they never really seemed to have lived worthy of emulation. They invariably seemed to live for others, for Black men or White; for children, or for parents; bereft, always it appeared, of an autonomous self" (Cudjoe, p. 11).

Two important breaks in tradition have come in the twentieth century. In 1945 Richard Wright published his autobiography, *Black Boy*, and touched off a debate that has not ended about the nature of the black experience in America. His hero is not a random member of a group who are victims of white oppression. The white oppressors are there, but the boy suffers as much from his black family who have become, under the heritage of slavery, sub-human in their hunger, fear, ignorance, superstition, brutality, and despair. By the miracle of books he is awakened to a life none of his family could comprehend. Years later, as a grown man, he saw the father who laughed at his hunger, saw him as a peasant of the soil and as an animal: "how chained were his actions and emotions to the direct, animalistic impulses of his withering body." The mature Wright pitied and forgave his father, but he left the lesson that he had to distance himself from his family or perish. Black writers especially have argued against his assertions:

> After I had outlived the shocks of childhood, after the habit of reflection had been born in me, I used to mull over the strange absence of real kindness in Negroes, how unstable was our tenderness, how lacking in genuine passion we were, how void of great hope, how timid our joy, how bare our traditions, how hollow our memories, how lacking we were in those intangible sentiments that bind man to man, and how shallow was even our despair (*Black Boy*, p. 45).

Much in *I Know Why the Caged Bird Sings* and in what Angelou has said about her writing shows her in opposition to Wright's dogma. Though the girl is lonely and hurt, she finds her way to survival in terms of the traditions of her family, her mother and her grandmother, not in opposition to them. She does remark that she knew few expressions of tenderness. The grandmother was embarrassed to discuss any emotions not associated with her religious faith; the mother imparted power but not tenderness. She describes her:

> . . . Vivian Baxter had no mercy. There was a saying in Oakland at the time which, if she didn't say it herself, explained her attitude. The saying was, 'Sympathy is next to shit in the dictionary, and I can't even read . . . She had the impartiality of nature, with the same lack of indulgence or clemency. (pp. 201–202)

In stressing her discovery of continuance of African ways among American blacks she argues with Wright's judgment that black traditions were "bare." In her description of her use of the mode autobiography, she says she was writing of one who typifies, not one who opposes or escapes the group.

I Know Why the Caged Bird Sings appeared in 1970. In the same year appeared Toni Morrison's *The Bluest Eye*, Alice Walker's *The Third Life of Grange Copeland*, Louise Meriwether's *Daddy Was a Numbers Runner*, Michele Wallace's Black *Macho and the Myth of Superwoman*, and Nikki Giovanni's *Black Feeling, Black Talk/Black Judgement*. In these and other notable works of the 1970's—Ntozake Shange's *For Colored Girls Who Have Considered Suicide/When the Rainbow is Enuf*—black woman writers have debated the effects of black sexism, and many have asserted that they must find their identity not merely in opposition to an oppressive white culture but in opposition to the traditions for the woman that the black culture imposes.

Angelou has put herself apart consistently from the movement of white women's liberation. Black women, she says, have never been as subservient within their community as white women in theirs: "White men, who are in effect their fathers, husbands, brothers, their sons, nephews and uncles, say to white women, or imply in any case: 'I don't really need you to run my institutions. I need you in certain places and in those places you must be kept—in the bedroom, in the kitchen, in the nursery, and on the pedestal.' Black women have never been told this." Though they have not occupied the pulpits, black women have been leaders in their communities, according to Angelou. She is pleased with the dialogue that these black women's works have begun. Though she has been criticized for including the rape in *I Know Why the Caged Bird Sings*, she says the whole truth must be told, and she says there is much truth still to be told of the male point of view of such works as *For Colored Girls Who Have Considered Suicide*.

Angelou's works and words point to her conviction that the black tradition is adequate and good, that black women emerge from it triumphant and strong. Critics have noted that absence of significant men in her autobiographies, and she certainly has been, since her years of teen-age motherhood, a woman who had to survive on her own strengths. In the midst of the debate of the 70's over the place of women in black culture, she affirmed that, subservient to no one, she was willing and honored to "serve." As one who had to work to survive, she says she has always been "liberated":

> I am so "liberated" that except on rare occasions my husband does not walk into the house without seeing his dinner prepared. He does not have to concern himself about a dirty house, I do that, for myself but also for my husband. I think it is important

to make that very clear. I think there is something gracious and graceful about serving. Now, unfortunately, or rather the truth is, our history in this country has been the history of the servers and because we were forced to serve and because dignity was absolutely drained from the servant, for anyone who serves in this country, black or white, is looked upon with such revilement, they are held in such contempt while that is not true in other parts of the world. In Africa it is a great honor to serve . . ."

I Know Why the Caged Bird Sings is sixteen years old now, the experience it recounts more than forty years old. Yet nothing, it seems, could be more timely.

It is an admirable story; and it is not typical. Typically the black girl who has no permanent father in her home, who is shuffled between mother and grandmother, city and country, who is raped at eight, a mother at sixteen, who supports her child without help from its father or from her own mother, with odd jobs, waitress, barmaid, prostitute—typically such girls do not become *Ladies Home Journal's* Woman of the Year for Communications or Reynolds Professor at Wake Forest or recipients of a dozen honorary degrees. For all Angelou's heroic assertion that the black woman emerges victorious from oppression and abuse, most of them do not. They are not equipped to succeed by any of the traditions here laid out, not that of the dominant white bourgeoisie which taught a generation of Southern women, black and white, to sew and crochet and be debutantes; not that of the pious black churchwomen who look for reward and vindication in the next life; not that of the black streets where one of her mother's boy friends was kicked to death, another one shot, where Angelou once herself took a pistol to the home of a boy who had threatened her son. Few black women have had work so well for them the swift vengeance outside the law; they have been victims of lawlessness as cruel as the law which first held them oppressed and then neglected their victimization.

Angelou knows it is a heroic, not typical model. The dedication, you remember, is to her son and to "all the strong Black birds of promise who defy the odds and gods."

One last note: Bearing the emphasis on family with tradition we have seen common to Southern literature, this book bears no mark of the provincialism of which not only Southern literature but much American literature of recent decades, especially the literature of American women, has been accused.

You have probably been reading, as I have, of the recent writers' congress, PEN, in New York. The complaints of non-American writers,

Salmon Rushdie, Nadine Gordimer, were loud that ours has become a literature of the misunderstood individual. It abounds in complaints and self-centered pre-occupations—will the heroine, like Gail Godwin's Odd Woman, achieve orgasm; it finds little room for the hunger of the children of the world or for the brutalities of police states.

Artistically Maya Angelou may err on the side of didacticism but she is free of exaggerated self-concern. The voice in the story shifts, from the girl of limited experience and perspective to that of the writer who speaks with the authority of truths gleaned from the traditions as diverse as Shakespeare and Ghanian folk tale. By her work she has not only contributed to but expanded the American literary tradition and the perspective from which this literature views—and serves—the world.

CAROL E. NEUBAUER

Displacement and Autobiographical Style in Maya Angelou's The Heart of a Woman

When Maya Angelou started her autobiographical series in 1970 with *I Know Why the Caged Bird Sings*, she naturally chose her childhood as the organizing principle of her first volume. The story of *Caged Bird* begins when the three-year-old Angelou and her four-year-old brother, Bailey, are turned over to the care of their paternal grandmother in Stamps, Arkansas, and it ends with the birth of her son when she is seventeen years old. The next two volumes, *Gather Together In My Name* (1974) and *Singin' and Swingin' and Gettin' Merry Like Christmas* (1976), narrate Angelou's life along chronological lines for the most part, and one would expect that her most recent addition to the autobiographical sequence, *The Heart of a Woman* (1981), would proceed with the account of her career as entertainer, writer, and freedom fighter. In many ways, Angelou meets her readers' expectations as she follows her life forward chronologically in organizing the newest segment in the series. Yet it is interesting to note that at the beginning of *The Heart of a Woman*, as she continues the account of her son's youth, she returns to the story of her own childhood repeatedly. The references to her childhood serve partly to create a textual link for readers who might be unfamiliar with the earlier volumes and partly to emphasize the suggestive similarities between her own childhood and that of her son. Maya Angelou's overwhelming sense of displacement and instability is, ironically, her son's burden too.

The most significant similarity between their childhood years is the

From *Black American Literature Forum* 17:3. © 1983 by Saint Louis University. Reprinted by permission.

condition of displacement in a familial as well as a geographical sense. Both Angelou and Guy, her son, are displaced from their immediate families several times during their youth. They are placed in the care of relatives or family friends and are moved from neighborhood to neighborhood and state to state. In a brief flashback in the second chapter of *The Heart of a Woman*, the writer reminds us of the displacement which characterized her youth and links this aspect of her past with her son's present attitude. When Guy is fourteen, Angelou decides to move to New York. She does not bring Guy to New York until she has found a place for them to live, and when he arrives after a one-month separation, he initially resists her attempts to make a new home for them:

> The air between us [Angelou and Guy] was burdened with his aloof scorn. I understood him too well.
>
> When I was three my parents divorced in Long Beach, California, and sent me and my four-year-old brother, unescorted, to our paternal grandmother. We wore wrist tags which informed anyone concerned that we were Marguerite and Bailey Johnson, en route to Mrs. Annie Henderson in Stamps, Arkansas.
>
> Except for disastrous and mercifully brief encounters with each of them when I was seven, we didn't see our parents again until I was thirteen.

From this and similar encounters with Guy, Angelou learns that the continual displacement of her own childhood is something she cannot prevent from recurring in her son's life.

Rather than a unique cycle perpetuated only within her family, Angelou's individual story presents a clear pattern commonly shared and passed along to new generations continually. In fact she identifies her own situation and the threat of displacement as a common condition among black families in America and acknowledges the special responsibility of the black mother: "She questions whether she loves her children enough—or more terribly, does she love them too much? . . . In the face of these contradictions, she must provide a blanket of stability, which warms but does not suffocate, and she must tell her children the truth about the power of white power without suggesting that it cannot be challenged" (p. 37). Providing stability for the children as the family disintegrates is a virtually impossible task, not only for Angelou but for many women in similar situations. After the dissolution of the family, the single parent is often left with an overwhelming sense of guilt and inadequacy; and, for Angelou, the burden is all the more taxing, because she has been solely responsible for her son from the very beginning of his life.

In *The Heart of a Woman*, Angelou includes numerous anecdotes from Guy's youth which mirror problems she has also faced. These compelling accounts suggest the recurring pattern of displacement and rejection in the relationship between mother and child. Many times Angelou feels that she and her son are skating dangerously "on thin ice!" As a child, Guy expects his mother to offer him constant attention and affection as well as the basic requirements of food and shelter, for which Angelou must often work long hours at more than one job. Her babysitting expenses alone often consume a substantial part of her meager income.

Guy's needs, however, are not simple, and in addition to love, companionship, and the basic necessities, he frequently intimates that his mother should be responsible for order and security on a universal level as well. "My son expected warmth, food, housing, clothes and stability. He could be certain that no matter which way my fortune turned he would receive most of the things he desired. Stability, however, was not possible in my world; consequently it couldn't be possible in his" (p. 123). Angelou's sense of personal failure in caring adequately for Guy lingers for many years. Similarly his sense of disappointment and rejection is reinforced every time his mother brings a new man into their already tenuous relationship or suggests yet another relocation to enhance her professional or economic status.

As Angelou narrates selected events that illustrate the periods of displacement in Guy's life, she adapts elements from both fiction and fantasy. Although she is clearly working within the genre of autobiography, Angelou freely borrows from these two traditionally more imaginative types of writing. On numerous occasions in her earlier volumes, she has employed what has become a rather personalized autobiographical style, a method which integrates ingredients from diverse modes of writing and gracefully crosses over traditionally static generic lines. One of the most memorable uses of fantasy in all of Angelou's writing is found in *Caged Bird* and involves a visit to a racist dentist in Stamps. As a child, she imagines that her grandmother grows to gigantic height and instantly gains superhuman strength to retaliate against the bigoted dentist who refuses to treat Angelou. In *Heart of a Woman*, she combines fiction and fantasy with the more standard biographical or historical mode to capture the subtleties of her relationship with her son and to emphasize the apparent similarities between their lives.

Examples of fictionalization in *Heart of a Woman* are quite varied. They range from rather common techniques such as representational detail in description and reconstructed accounts of actual dialogue, to more specialized devices used to create a sense of history beyond the individual life story and to include other narratives from folklore within her own narrative. Each fictional technique contributes to the overall completeness and credibility of the autobiographical text.

In *Heart of a Woman*, Angelou deliberately strives to capture the individual conversational styles of her relatives and friends. In a sense, her friends and acquaintances become "characters" in the story of her life, and like any good writer of fiction, she attempts to make their conversations realistic and convincing. With some of the people who figure in her autobiography, there is no objective measure for credibility other than the reader's critical appreciation for life itself. If the conversant in question is not well-known beyond the scope of the autobiography, Angelou need only ensure that the dialogue attributed to the individual be consistent with his character as delineated in the text itself. Yet many of her friends and associates were either highly successful celebrities or popular political figures, and the conversations recorded in her life story have points of reference beyond the autobiographical text. In other words, readers can test the degree of verisimilitude in the recorded dialogues with either firsthand knowledge or secondhand sources of information about the celebrities' lives.

It is highly probable, for example, that many of Angelou's readers are already familiar with the rhetorical styles of Martin Luther King, Jr., and Malcolm X, and the popular lyrics of Billie Holiday. In fact the lives of these three people in such accounts as *Why We Can't Wait*, *The Autobiography of Malcolm X*, and *Lady Sings the Blues* have in many ways become part of our contemporary folk history. Angelou adds a personalized quality to her recollections of conversations with these individuals and many others. The record of their conversations in *Heart of a Woman* brings them to life again, because the autobiographer is sensitive to and even somewhat self-conscious about the accurate reconstruction of their individual styles.

Since memory is not infallible, fictionalization comes into play whenever the autobiographer reconstructs or, perhaps more correctly, recreates conversation. While the autobiographer relies on invention, he or she creates the illusion of an infallible memory that records exactly the feel of a place and the words spoken there. Thus, when Angelou narrates visits with Billie Holiday in Laurel Canyon, she takes care to imitate her rather flamboyant verbal style:

> . . . she [Billie Holiday] talked about Hawaii.
> "People love 'the islands, the islands.' Hell, all that shit is a
> bunch of water and a bunch of sand. So the sun shines all the

time. What the hell else is the sun supposed to do?"

"But didn't you find it beautiful? The soft air, the flowers, the palm trees and the people? The Hawaiians are so pretty.'

"They just a bunch of riggers. Niggers running around with no clothes on. And that music shit they play. Uhn, uhn." She imitated the sound of a ukulele.

"Naw, I'd rather be in New York. Everybody in New York City is a son of a bitch, but at least they don't pretend they're something else." (p. 9)

As much as Angelou is shocked by the first words that tumble out of the famous entertainer's mouth, she is moved by Holiday's sensitivity in communicating with a precocious young boy who would be offended by any "off-color" phrases. "She carefully avoided profanity and each time she slipped, she'd excuse herself to Guy, saying, 'It's just another bad habit I got'" (p. 13). Holiday and Guy soon develop a balanced rapport and thoroughly enjoy the little time they spend together. Guy exuberantly tells her about his adventures and the books he has read, while she in turn sings her sorrowful songs to him as she relaxes and finds solace in the company of the child. In a sense, the anecdotes about Billie Holiday in *Heart of a Woman* form a tribute to her, for as Angelou admits, "I would remember forever the advice of a lonely sick woman, with a waterfront mouth, who sang pretty songs to a twelve-year-old boy" (p. 17).

In addition to using fictional techniques in the reconstruction of dialogue, Angelou turns to fictionalization to create a sense of history larger than the story of her own life. In her description of her meeting with Malcolm X, for example, Angelou combines the re-creation of credible dialogue with historical references that go beyond her individual life. Again there are points of reference beyond the writer's account that measure its accuracy.

In one scene, Angelou and her close friend Rosa Guy, both representatives of the Cultural Association of Women of African Heritage, decide to call on Malcolm X to ask for his help in controlling a potential riot situation brought about by their United Nations demonstration to protest the death of Lumumba. The following dialogue demonstrates her talent for remembering and recording their conversation as precisely as possible:

I joined the telling, and we distributed our story equally, like the patter of a long-time vaudeville duo.

"We—CAWAH . . . "

"Cultural Association of Women of African Heritage."

"Wanted to protest the murder of Lumumba so we—"
"Planned a small demonstration. We didn't expect—"
"More than fifty people—"
"And thousands came."
"That told us that the people of Harlem are angry and that
they are more for Africa and Africans"
"than they ever let on . . . " (p. 167)

Face to face with Malcolm X, Angelou and her friend, both extremely
articulate women, are reduced to a stammering "vaudeville duo." The
stichomythic rhythm in the reconstructed conversation suggests the degree
of intimidation that the women experienced in the presence of Malcolm X.
The power of his personality causes their initial uneasiness, which soon turns
to disappointment as Malcolm X coolly refuses to involve his Muslim
followers in public demonstration.

Angelou's unsuccessful interview with the Harlem leader provides a
clear contrast with her first meeting with Martin Luther King. The larger
historical context of their exchange expands the personal perimeter of her
life story. At the time of her first conversation with King, Angelou has been
working as Northern Coordinator of the Southern Christian Leadership
Conference in New York. She has devoted the previous months to raising
funds, boosting membership, and organizing volunteer labor both in the
office and in the neighborhoods. When Dr. King pays his first visit to the
New York office during her tenure, she does not have advance notice of his
presence and rushes into her office one day after lunch to find him sitting at
her desk. They begin to talk about her background and eventually focus their
comments on her brother, Bailey:

> "Come on, take your seat back and tell me about yourself."
> . . . When I mentioned my brother Bailey, he asked what he
> was doing now.
> The question stopped me. He was friendly and
> understanding, but if I told him my brother was in prison, I
> couldn't be sure how long his understanding would last. I could
> lose my job. Even more important, I might lose his respect. Birds
> of a feather and all that, but I took a chance and told him Bailey
> was in Sing Sing.
> He dropped his head and looked at his hands. . . .
> "I understand. Disappointment drives our young men to
> some desperate lengths." Sympathy and sadness kept his voice
> low. "That's why we must fight and win. We must save the

Baileys of the world. And Maya, never stop loving him. Never give up on him. Never deny him. And remember, he is freer than those who hold him behind bars." (pp. 92-93)

Angelou appreciates King's sympathy, and of course shares his hope that their work will make the world more fair and free. She recognizes the undeniable effects of displacement on Bailey's life and fervently hopes that her son, who has not escaped the pain of displacement, will be spared any further humiliation and rejection.

When Angelou extends her personal narrative to include anecdotes about well-known entertainers or political figures, or observations about significant historical events, she necessarily fictionalizes the story of her past. Fictionalization is clearly at play on both a conscious and an unconscious level in the act of remembering and transcribing key events from her private life, but it becomes virtually inevitable in recording her subjective impressions about a public event or person. Whenever there is more than one account of an event, as there usually is in the public or historical context, comparisons reveal inconsistencies or discrepancies that are the product of varied individual response. Thus fictionalization occurs when Angelou includes other narratives within the narrative of her life. Each borrowed story is usually a sampling of folklore, but is told in a slightly different context to achieve a special effect within the autobiography.

One example of adapting borrowed narratives to illuminate her own story involves the folktale of Brer Rabbit. Several months after Angelou marries the South African freedom fighter Vusumzi Make, they decide to move from their apartment in New York to Cairo to facilitate Make's efforts to raise funds and political support for the cause. When they leave for Egypt with Guy, the family looks forward to a period untroubled by the abusive telephone threats that riddled the domestic peace of their lives together in New York. But although the threatening telephone calls end when they move to Cairo, Angelou finds a different restriction on her life that has little to do with political sanctions of the South African government: As the wife of a well-known activist, she ironically finds her own life less free and is not at liberty to find work for herself, because her husband prefers that she stay at home and devote her time fully to her responsibilities as housewife and mother.

After several months in Cairo, however, the Make family suffers financial restraints, and Angelou takes it upon herself to seek employment without her husband's knowledge. Through the help of a family friend, she is offered the job of Editor of *The Arab Observer*, a Cairo-based news journal with an international scope. Although she has not been trained professionally in journalism, Angelou accepts the position, partly to supplement the family income, but more importantly to meet the challenge of the job. The challenge of being Editor is a significant one, not only because of the demanding and diverse responsibilities but, more critically, because as a black American woman working with a male staff in a country deeply influenced by the Islamic faith, Angelou has to prove herself on more than one level.

The conditions in her office at first are less than friendly. when Angelou gives an account of the relief she experienced when moved from her centrally located desk into a rather secluded library, she borrows a popular tale from Joel Chandler Harris' Brer Rabbit:

> Finally, when the farmer had the rabbit turning at a fast speed, he pointed him toward the briar patch and let go. Brer Rabbit landed on his feet. His eyes were dry and bright. His ears perked up and waved. Brer Rabbit grinned at the farmer, his teeth shining white as buttermilk. He said, "Home, at last. Home at last. Great God Almighty, I'm home at last."
>
> I smiled sweetly as the men shoved and pulled my desk into the library. When they left, and I stood before the crowded book shelves, reading unfamiliar titles and the names of authors unknown to me, still I felt just like Brer Rabbit in the briar patch. (p. 233)

Angelou equates her delight in her move to the library with Brer Rabbit's relief at being tossed into the briar patch by the farmer. Both are victims, in a sense, of their situations yet both use their native wit and resourcefulness to overcome debilitating odds. The books in the library are written in English and are just what Angelou needs to supplement her knowledge of international politics and the Arab world. Moreover, by borrowing the Brer Rabbit narrative, Angelou makes an implicit comparison between her own position as a black American woman in an African, Islamic, male-oriented world and the inhumane conditions of black Americans in slavery. Finally, by including one of the earliest examples of folk literature about blacks in America, Angelou places her own narrative within the ranks of an established folk tradition.

Just as her experiences as a black American in Africa call to mind Brer Rabbit on occasion, so she recalls the stories of several slave heroines while attending an informal gathering of African women in London. All of the women present are the wives of political activists in the struggle to end apartheid and second-class citizenship for black Africans. Although their national backgrounds are quite different, they share the same sense of

frustration and ineffectualness in comparison with their husbands, who
ironically enjoy more autonomy in the fight for freedom. To ease their sense
of uselessness, they gather one day in the home of Mrs. Oliver Tambo, the
wife of the leader of the African National Congress. Here the women narrate
traditional tales from African folklore. Although Angelou initially feels
somewhat estranged from the spontaneous ceremony, she is soon moved to
share folktales from the tradition of slave narratives concerning women who
led the fight for freedom in America.

Her first story narrates the history of Harriet Tubman, a model of the
strong black women at the heart of American history, a woman who fought
against devastating odds and suffered extraordinary personal sacrifice to free
many of her people. Tubman is, therefore, an appropriate figure to celebrate
in an international group of black women. Tubman, Angelou tells them,
"stood on free ground, above a free sky, hundreds of miles from the chains
and lashes of slavery and said, 'I must go back. With the help of God I will
bring others to freedom,' and . . . although suffering brain damage from a
slaver's blow, she walked back and forth through the lands of bondage time
after time and brought hundreds of her people to freedom" (p. 137). Pleased
with the success of her first tale, Angelou follows the inspiring story of
Harriet Tubman with an even more dramatic presentation of the heroism of
Sojourner Truth. Once again she selects the figure of a fearless black
American woman who devoted her life to end slavery and to educate both
Northerners and Southerners about the responsibilities of freedom.
Sojourner Truth, like Harriet Tubman, is a fitting example of the essential
strength of black American women to share with a group of African women
celebrating the same heroic characteristics in their ancestors. The anecdote
relates an equal rights meeting in the 1800s at which Truth addressed the
group and was accused by a white man of being a man dressed as a woman:

> "Ain't I a woman? I have suckled your babes at this breast."
> Here she put her large hands on her bodice. Grabbing the cloth
> she pulled. The threads gave way, the blouse and her
> undergarments parted and her huge tits hung, pendulously free.
> She continued, her face unchanging and her voice never
> faltering, "And ain't I a woman?"
> When I finished the story, my hands tugging at the buttons
> of my blouse, the African women stood applauding, stamping
> their feet and crying. Proud of their sister whom they had not
> known a hundred years before. (p. 138)

The stories about Sojourner Truth and Harriet Tubman, like the
folktale of Brer Rabbit, enlarge the scope of Angelou's autobiography and

bring certain historical points of reference to the story of one person's life. Readers come to understand *Heart of a Woman* not only through the avenues of her life opened in the text but through the samplings of folklore that are included as well. Fictionalization comes into play as Angelou adapts these borrowed narratives and anecdotes to illustrate the theme of displacement in her life and her son's.

I have shown that Angelou adapts fictional techniques in *Heart of a Woman* to make her life story fully realistic and convincing, and to supplement the personal scope with the larger historical context. In addition Angelou uses elements of fantasy to illustrate disappointments and defeats she has experienced in life and to reveal the complexity of her relationship with her son. Her use of fantasy can be divided into two types: the narration of a fantasy that ends in illusion and suggests the autobiographer's somewhat ironic stance in examining her past and the narration of a fantasy that becomes reality and emphasizes her inability to protect her son and herself from harmful influences. With both types of fantasy, the writer stresses the importance of imagination when a situation does not measure up to one's expectations.

One of the most important examples of the first type of fantasy concerns Angelou's prospects for marriage at various times in her life. She includes her unrealistic hopes for her impending marriages to demonstrate how firmly she had believed in the American dream of stability through marriage and family. Even in the earlier *Singin' and Swingin' and Gettin' Merry Like Christmas*, Angelou had accounted for her illusory belief that she had finally met the man of her dreams who would give her everything she had always lacked—love, domestic tranquility, security, children, and an attractive house in the suburbs modeled after *Better Homes and Gardens*:

> At last I was a housewife, legally a member of that enviable tribe of consumers whom security made as fat as butter and who under no circumstances considered living by bread alone, because their husbands brought home the bacon. I had a son, a father for him, a husband and a pretty home for us to live in. My life began to resemble a Good Housekeeping advertisement. I cooked well-balanced meals and molded fabulous jello desserts. My floors were dangerous with daily applications of wax and our furniture slick with polish.

When Angelou describes her fantasy about marriage and its power to bring normalcy and stability to her life, whether in *Singin' and Swingin'* or *Heart of a Woman*, she uses an ironic point of view to suggest how much she had yet to learn about marriage. Her ironic stance, thereby, fosters understanding on the part of the reader.

In *Heart of a Woman*, Angelou stresses the irony in her present perspective by juxtaposing her fantasized notion of marriage with the way two relationships actually develop. She carefully exposes her illusory hopes and underscores her naïveté with the actual disappointment she experienced. While working in New York, Angelou meets Thomas Allen, a bail bondsman, whom she plans to marry in order to bring stability into her life and a father into Guy's. For some years, she has looked for a strong, honest man who, ideally, would help her shoulder the responsibility of raising Guy. She privately imagines the assumed advantages of marrying Thomas until she has convinced herself of her dream:

> I was getting used to the idea and even liking it. We'd buy a nice house out on Long Island, where he had relatives. I would join a church and some local women's volunteer organizations. Guy wouldn't mind another move if he was assured that it was definitely the last one. I would let my hair grow out and get it straightened and wear pretty hats with flowers and gloves and look like a nice colored woman from San Francisco. (p. 102)

But even before the fantasy becomes an illusion, Angelou begins to distrust her dream-like wishes. Her friends and his family caution them not to marry, and she even feels a "twinge which tried to warn me that I should stop and do some serious thinking" (p. 103).

Angelou, however, ignores this annoying suspicion as long as possible, until, one evening when Allen is at her home for dinner, she suddenly realizes what her real future with him would be like:

> At home, Guy watched television and Thomas read the sports pages while I cooked dinner. I knew that but for my shocking plans, we were acting out the tableau of our future. Into eternity, Guy would be in his room, laughing at *I Love Lucy* and Thomas would be evaluating the chances of an atthelete [sic] or a national baseball team, and I would be leaning over the stove, preparing food for the "shining dinner hour." Into eternity. (p. 124)

In spite of this rather sobering premonition, Angelou does not make her decision to break her engagement with Thomas, until she meets Vus Make, who convinces her that she would be in a better position to offer her gift of humanism to others if she were married to a South African political figure rather than to a bail bondsman.

Although Vus Make's goals are quite different from Thomas Allen's, Angelou experiences the same belief in a perfect fantasy future with her prospective husband—and its dissolution. Part of her imagined future would provide her with the same domestic security she had hoped would develop from other relationships. "I was getting a husband, and a part of that gift was having someone to share responsibilities and guilt" (p. 131). Yet her hopes are even more idealistic than usual, inasmuch as she imagines herself participating in the liberation of South Africa as Vus Make's wife: "With my courage added to his own, he would succeed in bringing the ignominious white rule in South Africa to an end. If I didn't already have the qualities he needed, then I would just develop them. Infatuation made me believe in my ability to create myself into my lover's desire" (p. 123). In reality Angelou is only willing to go so far in recreating herself to meet her husband's desires and is all too soon frustrated with her role as Make's wife. He does not want her to work, but is unable to support his expensive tastes, as well as his family, on his own. The family is evicted from their New York apartment just before they leave for Egypt, and they soon face similar problems in Cairo. Their marriage dissolves after some months despite Angelou's efforts to hold her own as Editor of *The Arab Observer*. In her autobiography she underscores the illusory nature of her fantasy about marriage to show how her perspective has shifted over the years and how much understanding she has gained about life in general. Fantasy, for Angelou, is a form of truth-telling and a way to present subtle truths about her life to her readers.

The second type of fantasy in *Heart of a Woman* is born out in reality rather than in illusion, as is the case with her expectations for marriage. One of the most important uses of the second kind of fantasy involves a sequence that demonstrates how much Angelou fears for Guy's safety throughout his youth. Although her imagination is more sensitive than are the imaginations of most, the recurrent vision of one's child meeting with unexpected danger is common to most parents. Angelou organizes her repetitive fantasies about Guy into a pattern in her autobiography to explain the guilt and inadequacy she often felt in her role as mother.

Throughout her life, she strives to balance the responsibilities of motherhood and the demands of her career as a professional entertainer and writer. Since she has the primary responsibility for raising Guy without a husband and earning an income adequate to meet their basic needs, Angelou is often faced with an impossible situation. She cannot spend as much time with her son as she would like and hold a full-time job at the same time. Thus she is often caught in a situation for which no solution is satisfactory, and she cannot help but suffer from the paradox of being both a victim and a perpetrator of the cycle of displacement.

The first example of a fantasy which involves a threat to Guy's life relates to his mother's career as a professional singer. Although Angelou has vowed to give up the life of an entertainer permanently, she cannot resist an invitation to perform at the opening of the Gate of Horn in Chicago. She naturally has second thoughts about leaving Guy on his own, but cannot turn down the opportunity to earn enough money in two weeks to pay two months' rent. Before leaving New York, she makes arrangements with her close friend John Killens to watch over Guy, even though he is already quite independent and often resents the implication that he needs care or guidance. She also hires an older black woman to stay at her home and cook for Guy.

As she is checking out of her hotel in Chicago, Angelou is called to the phone to hear Killens' voice tell her that there has been trouble. His first words are enough to awaken her deepest fears and replay an all-too-familiar scenario:

> The dread, closer than a seer's familiar, which lived sucking off my life, was that something would happen to my only son. He would be stolen, kidnapped by a lonely person who, seeing his perfection, would be unable to resist. He would be struck by an errant bus, hit by a car out of control. He would walk a high balustrade, showing his beauty and coordination to a girl who was pretending disinterest. His foot would slip, his body would fold and crumble, he would fall fifty feet and someone would find my phone number. I would be minding my own business and a stranger would call me to the phone.
>
> "Hello?"
>
> A voice would say, "There's been trouble."
>
> My nightmare never went further. I never knew how serious the accident was, or my response. And now real life pushed itself through the telephone. (p. 75)

"Real life," in the form of Killens' voice, assures her that Guy is now safe at his home but does not tell her any related details on the telephone, thus allowing her fantasy to grow. Back in New York, she learns that her son has received a threat from a local gang, because the leader's girlfriend has accused Guy of insulting her. As soon as she returns and has a chance to survey the circumstances, Angelou confronts the gang leader directly and warns him against further contact with her son. Although Guy is never actually harmed by the gang, his mother's fantasized nightmare has been brought a step closer to "real life."

A second segment in the pattern of fantasy concerning danger threatening Guy's life relates to the telephone harassment the Make family experiences before their move to Cairo. Shortly after her marriage to Make, Angelou begins to receive threatening phone calls during the day when neither Vus nor Guy is at home. Most concern her husband and, according to him, are placed by people working for the South African government. Initially Angelou responds to all of the telephone calls as if they were true, but gradually learns to distance herself from the immediate shock and lingering fear. Even changing their telephone number does not put an end to the calls; and, occasionally, the unidentified voice informs her that her son has met with unexpected danger and will not be returning home. These calls, of course, nurture her recurrent fantasy about Guy's safety and show the vulnerability she feels as a mother trying to protect her child from any form of danger:

> One afternoon I answered the telephone and was thumped into a fear and subsequent rage so dense that I was made temporarily deaf.
>
> "Hello, Maya Make?" Shreds of a Southern accent still hung in the white woman's voice.
>
> "Yes? Maya Make speaking." I thought the woman was probably a journalist or a theater critic, wanting an interview from Maya Angelou Make, the actress.
>
> "I'm calling about Guy." My mind shifted quickly from a pleasant anticipation to apprehension.
>
> "Are you from his school? What is the matter?"
>
> "No, I'm at Mid-town Hospital. I'm sorry but there's been a serious accident. We'd like you to come right away. Emergency ward." (p. 193)

Angelou does not stop to think about the recent telephone threats until she arrives at the emergency ward to discover that Guy is not there. A telephone call to his school soon assures her that he is safe in his classroom and that she has been the victim of the South African threats and her own fear for her son's life.

Yet not all threats to Guy's life end as harmlessly as the challenge from the gang and the anonymous phone calls. In Accra, where Angelou and Guy go after her marriage with Vus Make deteriorates, she receives another shocking intrusion from "real life." The difference between this warning of danger and all others in the pattern is that this threat brings fantasy to the level of reality. The threat is neither speculative nor alleged, but real.

Just a few days after their arrival in Ghana, some friends invite Angelou and Guy to a picnic. Although his mother declines, Guy immediately accepts the invitation in a show of independence. On the way home from the day's outing, her son is seriously injured in an automobile accident. Even though he has had very little experience driving, Guy is asked to drive, because his host is too intoxicated to operate the car himself. At the time of the collision, the car is at a standstill.

The pair's return delayed, Angelou, before long, is once again terrified by her recurrent nightmare concerning Guy's safety. This time, however, the fantasy becomes reality:

> Korle Bu's emergency ward was painfully bright. I started down the corridor and found myself in a white tunnel, interrupted by a single loaded gurney, resting against a distant wall. I walked up to the movable table and saw my son, stretched his full length under white sheets. His rich golden skin paled to ash-grey. His eyes closed and his head at an unusual angle.
>
> I took my arm away from Alice's grasp and told Katie to stop her stupid snuffling. When they backed away, I looked at my son, my real life. He was born to me when I was seventeen. I had taken him away from my mother's house when he was two months old, and except for a year I spent in Europe without him, and a month when he was stolen by a deranged woman, we had spent our lives together. My grown life lay stretched before me, stiff as a pine board, in a strange country, blood caked on his face and clotted on his clothes. (p. 263)

Although Angelou has never been to Korle Bu Hospital, the emergency ward is painfully familiar. The crisis becomes all the more urgent because they are as yet unaccustomed to the language and have very little available money. Angelou captures the depth of her fear by calling her injured, immobile son, "my real life," "my grown life." In this sequence of fantasy moving to the level of reality, the autobiographer suggests the vulnerability she felt in her role as a mother with full responsibility for the well-being of her only child. In a new country, estranged from her husband with no immediate prospects for employment, Angelou possesses very little control over her life or her son's safety. After the accident in Ghana, Guy is not only striving for independence from his mother but for life itself.

The complex nature of her relationship with her son is at the heart of this most recent of Angelou's autobiographical volumes. At the end, Guy is seventeen and has just passed the matriculation exams at the University of

Ghana. The last scene pictures Guy driving off to his new dormitory room with several fellow university students. The conclusion of *Heart of a Woman* announces a new beginning for Angelou and hope for her future relationship with Guy. In this sense, the newest volume in the series follows the pattern established by the conclusions of the earlier volumes. *Caged Bird* ends with the birth of Guy, *Gather Together* with the return to her mother's home in San Francisco after regaining her innocence through the lessons of a drug addict, and *Singin' and Swingin'* with the reunion of mother and son in a paradisiacal setting of a Hawaiian resort. The final scene of *Heart of a Woman* suggests that the future will bring more balance between dependence and independence in their relationship and that both will have significant personal successes as their lives begin to take different courses. Although Guy has assumed that he has been fully "grown up" for years, they have at last reached a point where they can treat each other as adults and allow one another the chance to live independently. Many of Angelou's victories are reflected in Guy in the last scene, for, although Guy is the same age she is at the end of *Caged Bird*, his young life promises many more opportunities and rewards as a result of his mother's perseverance and her belief "that life loved the person who dared to live it." Moreover, Angelou shares Guy's fresh sense of liberation; she too is embarking on a new period of strength and independence as she begins her life yet again— on her own and in a new land. It is from this position of security that Maya Angelou looks back to record her life story and to compensate for the years of distance and displacement through the autobiographical act.

Chronology

1928   April 4, Marguerite Johnson is born.

1931   Sent to live with their grandmother in Stamps, Arkansas.

1936   Raped by her mother's boyfriend, becomes mute.

1940   Graduates with honors from Lafayette Country Training School.

1944   Becomes San Francisco's first black streetcar conductor; graduates from high school; gives birth to son.

1952   Marries Tosh Angelos.

1954   Sings at Purple Onion nightclub.

1954-55   Tours Europe with *Porgy and Bess*.

1959   Runs New York office of the Southern Christian Leadership Conference.

1960   Helps produce benefit, *Cabaret for Freedom*, for SCLC and stars in *The Blacks*.

1961   Moves to Egypt with Vusumzi Make.

1963   Moves to Ghana, working at the University of Ghana.

1968   Writes and produces a ten-part PBS television series, *Black, Blues, Black*.

1970   Publishes first autobiography, *I Know Why the Caged Bird Sings.*

1971   Publishes first book of poetry, *Just Give Me a Cool Drink of Water 'Fore I Diiie.*

1972   Writes first screenplay, *Georgia, Georgia.*

1973   Marries Paul Du Feu and debuts on Broadway in *Look Away.*

1976   Publishes second autobiography, *Singin' and Swingin' and Gettin' Merry Like Christmas.*

1977   Plays Kunta Kinte's grandmother in television mini-series *Roots.*

1978   Publishes book of poetry, *And Still I Rise.*

1980   Divorces Paul Du Feu.

1981   Publishes third autobiography, *The Heart of a Woman.*

1982   Appointed Reynolds Professor of American Studies at Wake Forest University.

1986   Publishes fourth autobiography, *All God's Children Need Traveling Shoes.*

1993   Reads "On the Pulse of Morning" at President Clinton's inauguration.

1995   Reads poems at 50th anniversary of United Nations and Million Man March.

1997   Publishes *Even the Stars Look Lonesome* and *From a Black Woman to a Black Man.*

2002   Publishes *A Song Flung Up To Heaven.*

Works by Maya Angelou

I Know Why the Caged Bird Sings, 1969.
Just Give Me a Cool Drink of Water 'Fore I Diiie, 1971.
Gather Together in My Name, 1974.
Oh Pray My Wings Are Gonna Fit Me Well, 1975.
Singin' and Swingin' and Gettin' Merry Like Christmas, 1976.
And Still I Rise, 1978.
The Heart of a Woman, 1981.
All God's Children Need Traveling Shoes, 1986.
Shaker, Why Don't You Sing, 1983.
Now Sheba Sings the Song, 1987.
I Shall Not Be Moved, 1990.
Life Doesn't Frighten Me, 1993.
"On The Pulse of Morning," 1993.
Wouldn't Take Nothing for My Journey Now, 1993.
Complete Collected Poems of Maya Angelou, 1994.
My Painted House, My Friendly Chicken and Me, 1994.
A Brave and Startling Truth, 1995.
Phenomenal Woman: Four Poems for Women, 1995.
Kofi and His Magic, 1996.
Even the Stars Look Lonesome, 1997.
From a Black Woman to a Black Man, 1997.

PLAYS AND SCREENPLAYS

Cabaret for Freedom, 1960
The Least of These, 1966
Gettin' Up Stayed on My Mind, 1967.
Georgia, Georgia, 1972.
All Day Long, 1974.
Ajax, 1974.
And Still I Rise, 1976.
Moon on a Rainbow Shawl, 1988.
A Song Flung Up to Heaven, 2002.

Works about Maya Angelou

Angelou, Maya. *I Know Why the Caged Bird Sings*. New York: Random House, 1969.

———. *Gather Together in My Name*. New York: Random House, 1974.

———. *Singin' and Swingin' and Gettin' Merry Like Christmas*. New York: Random House, 1976.

———. *The Heart of a Woman*. New York: Bantam Books, 1981.

———. *All God's Children Need Traveling Shoes*. New York: Random House, 1986.

———. *Wouldn't Take Nothing for My Journey Now*. New York: Random House 1993.

———. *The Complete Collected Poems of Maya Angelou*. New York: Random House, 1994.

Arensberg, Liliane K. "Death as Metaphor of Self in *I Know Why the Caged Bird Sings*." *CLA Journal* 20:2 (December 1976): 273–91.

Bloom, Harold, ed. *Modern Critical Interpretations: I Know Why the Caged Bird Sings*. Philadelphia: Chelsea House Publishers, 1998.

———. *Modern Critical Views: Maya Angelou*. Philadelphia: Chelsea House Publishers, 1999.

Braxton, Joanne M. "A Song of Transcendence: Maya Angelou." *Black Women Writing Autobiography: A Tradition Within a Tradition*. Philadelphia: Temple University, 1989.

Bertolino, James. "Maya Angelou Is Three Writers: *I Know Why the Caged Bird Sings*." *Censored Books, Critical Viewpoints*. Nicholas J. Karolides, Lee Burress, and John M. Kean, eds. Metuchen, NJ: Scarecrow Press, 1993.

Butterfield, Stephen. "Autobiographies of Black Women: Ida Wells, Maya Angelou, Anne Moody," *Black Autobiography in America*. Amherst: University of Massachusetts Press, 1974.

Challener, Daniel D. "When a Whole Village Raises a Child: *I Know Why the Caged Bird Sings*." *Stories of Resilience in Childhood: The Narratives of Maya Angelou, Maxine Hong Kingston, Richard Rodriguez, John Edgar Wideman, and Tobias Wolff*. New York: Garland Publishing, Inc., 1997.

Cudjoe, Selwyn R. "Maya Angelou and the Autobiographical Statement." *Black Women Writers (1950-1980): A Critical Evaluation*. New York: Bantam, 1984.

Davies, Carole Boyce. *Black Women, Writing, and Identity*. London: Routledge Press, 1994.

Elliot, Jeffrey M., ed. *Conversations with Maya Angelou*. Jackson: University Press of Mississippi, 1989.

Georgoudaki, Ekaterini. *Race, Gender, and Class Perspectives in the Works of Maya Angelou, Gwendolyn Brooks, Rita Dove, Nikki Giovanni, and Audre Lorde*. Thessaloniki: Aristotle University of Thessaloniki, 1991.

Gilbert, Susan. "Maya Angelou's *I Know Why the Caged Bird Sings*: Paths to Escape." *Mount Olive Review* 1:1 (Spring 1987): 39–50.

Gillespie, Marcia Ann. "Maya Angelou: Lessons in Living." *Essence*. Dec. 1992, 48 (5).

Hagen, Lyman B. *Heart of a Woman, Mind of a Writer, and Soul of a Poet*. New York: University Press of America, Inc, 1997.

Hazynes. Karima A. "Maya Angelou: Prime-Time Poet." *Ebony*, April 1993, 68 (3).

Hord, Fred Lee. "Someplace to Be a Black Girl" *Reconstructing Memory: Black Literary Criticism*. Chicago: Third World Press, 1991.

Kellaway, Kate, "Poet for the New America." *The Observer*, Jan. 24, 1993.

Kelly, Ken. "Maya Angelou: A Celebrated Poet Issues a Call to Arms to the Nation's Artists." *Mother Jones*, May–June 1995, 22 (4).

———."Maya Angelou's Invitation to Write Inaugural Poem Reflects Nation's Change." *Jet*, Dec. 21, 1992, 16.

Kent, George E. "Maya Angelou's I Know Why the Caged Bird Sings and the Black Autobiographical Tradition," *African American Autobiography: A Collection of Critical Essays*. Prentice Hall, 1993.

Kinnamon, Kenneth. "Call and Response: Intertexuality in Two Autobiographical Works by Richard Wright and Maya Angelou." *Studies in Black American Literature, Vol. II: Belief vs. Theory in Black American Literary Criticism.* Joe Weixlmann and Chester J. Fontenot, eds. Groonewood, FL: Penkevill Publishing Co., 1986.

Kite, Patricia. *Maya Angelou.* Minneapolis: Lerner Publications, 1999.

Kraft, Marion. "'Deep River, My Home Is Over Jordan': The African Experience of Maya Angelou." *The African Continuum and Contemporary African American Women Writers: Their Literary Presence and Ancestral Past.* New York: Peter Lang, 1995.

Lindberg-Seyersted, Brita. "Maya Angelou and the Homeland: One African-American Woman's Encounter with Africa." *Black and Female: Essays on Writing by Black Women in the Diaspora.* Oslo: Scandinavian University Press, 1994.

Lionnet, Françoise. "Con Artists and Storytellers: Maya Angelou's Problematic Sense of Audience." *Autobiographical Voices: Race, Gender, Self-Portraiture.* Ithaca: Cornell University Press, 1989.

Lupton, Mary Jane. *Maya Angelou: A Critical Companion.* London: Greenwood Press, 1998.

———. "Singing the Black Mother: Maya Angelou and Autobiographical Continuity." *Black American Literature Forum* 24:2 (Summer 1990): 257–76.

McCurry, Myra K. "Role-Playing As Art in Maya Angelou's 'Caged Bird'." *South Atlantic Bulletin* 41:2 (May 1976).

McPherson, Dolly Aimee. "Autobiography As the Evocation of the Spirit." In *Order out of Chaos: The Autobiographical Works of Maya Angelou.* New York: Peter Lang, 1989.

———. "The Significance of Maya Angelou." *Order out of Chaos: The Autobiographical Works of Maya Angelou.* New York: Peter Lang, 1989.

Meroney, John. "The Real Maya Angelou." *The American Spectator*, March 1993, 68.

Moore, Opal. "Learning to Live: When the Caged Bird Breaks from the Cage." In *Censored Books: Critical Viewpoints.* Nicholas J. Karolides, Lee Burress, and John M. Kean, eds. Metuchen, NJ: Scarecrow Press, 1993.

Neubauer, Carol E. "Displacement and Autobiographical Style in Maya Angelou's Heart of a Woman." *Black American Literature Forum* 17:3 (Fall 1983): 123–29.

————. "Maya Angelou: Self and a Song of Freedom in the Southern Tradition." *Southern Women Writers: The New Generation.* Tuscaloosa: University of Alabama Press, 1990.

O'Neale, Sondra. "Reconstruction of the Composite Self: New Images of Black Women in Maya Angelou's Continuing Autobiography." *Black Women Writers (1950–1980): A Critical Evaluation.* Mari Evans, ed. New York: Bantam, 1984.

Ramsey, Priscilla R. "Transcendence: The Poetry of Maya Angelou." *A Current Bibliography on African Affairs* 17:2 (1984–85): 139–153.

Smith, Sidonie Ann. "The Song of the Caged Bird: Maya Angelou's Quest for Self-Acceptance." *Southern Humanities Review* 7:4 (Fall 1973).

Sobran, Joseph. "Ecstasy on the Mall." *National Review*, Feb. 15, 1993, 34 (3).

Tennille, Norton F. "A Rock, a River, a Tree / a Poetic Controversy." *Harper's Magazine*, March 1994, 28 (3).

WEB SITES

www.mayaangelou.com/

www.poets.org/poets/poets.cfm?prmID=88

www.csustan.edu/english/reuben/pal/chap10/angelou.html

www.math.buffalo.edu/~sww/angelou/angelou.html

Contributors

HAROLD BLOOM is Sterling Professor of the Humanities at Yale University and Henry W. and Albert A. Berg Professor of English at the New York University Graduate School. He is the author of over 20 books, including *Shelly's Mythmaking* (1959), *The Visionary Company* (1961), *Blake's Apocalypse* (1963), *Yeats* (1970), *A Map of Misreading* (1975), *Kabbalah and Criticism* (1975), *Agon: Toward a Theory of Revisionism* (1982), *The American Religion* (1992), *The Western Canon* (1994), and *Omens of Millennium: The Gnosis of Angels, Dreams, and Resurrection* (1996). *The Anxiety of Influence* (1973) sets forth Professor Bloom's provocative theory of the literary relationships between the great writers and their predecessors. His most recent books include *Shakespeare: The Invention of the Human*, a 1998 National Book Award finalist, and *How to Read and Why*, which was published in 2000. In 1999, Professor Bloom received the prestigious American Academy of Arts and Letters Gold Medal for Criticism.

CINDY DYSON is a freelance writer who lives in Montana. She has written several books and many magazine articles.

RACHEL THOMAS lives in New Haven, CT where she works as a freelance writer. She studied literature at Yale University and wrote her thesis under the direction of Professor Bloom.

Susan Gilbert is a Professor of English literature at Meredith College where her focus is on twentieth century literature, Southern literature, women's literature, and world literature.

Carol E. Neubauer is a member of the Department of English and Foreign Language at Bradley University. She has written extensively on Maya Angelou and other writers in journals such as *Black American Literature Forum*, *Journal of Modern African Studies*, *MELUS*, *World Literature Written in English*, and *Massachusetts Review*. Her recent work includes a study of Chinese women writers.

Index